GREAT MOMENTS IN FOOTBALL

EDITED BY
MARTIN TYLER

MACDONALD & JANE'S, LONDON

The editor wishes to thank Doreen Gilbert, for typing the manuscript and Lionel Francis, for helping with research.

**Published by the Queen Anne Press Division of
  Macdonald & Jane's Publishers Limited,
  Paulton House,
  8 Shepherdess Walk,
  London N1 7LW**

Printed and bound in England by
C. Nicholls & Company Ltd.,
The Philips Park Press, Manchester.

CONTENTS

A HORSE NAMED BILLY

The story of the first Wembley Cup final

It probably comes as a surprise to the great majority of fans on football terraces today to learn that, for half its life, the FA Cup final was *not* played at Wembley. The ritual that has become so familiar, the crowds flocking towards the twin towers of the stadium, the singing of Abide With Me, the teams coming out together, are all really rather modern innovations.

In fact on its 50th birthday, in 1922, the Cup final had ended up in the dreary and inappropriate surroundings of Stamford Bridge. A mere 53,000 people turned up to see Huddersfield defeat Preston 1-0 with a last-minute penalty in a game so poor and so violent that the FA afterwards complained to both clubs about their behaviour.

Stamford Bridge was, and in many ways still is, woefully inadequate for a big event, and the FA knew that they would have to move their showpiece. Crystal Palace, the pre-World War I venue, was due to be released by the army in 1923. But despite its vast capacity, much of the crowd had invariably been too far away to see very much in the shallowly banked and uncovered arena.

The solution was provided by the British Empire Exhibition – a massive circus, public relations exercise, and patriotic outpouring to celebrate the supposed height of an Empire which was already waning away. Part of the scheme was for a stadium, the largest specially built in England (though Hampden Park was still bigger) to house major events. The site chosen for the Exhibition area was at Wembley, then a sleepy suburb far from the bustle of central London – although it was less than ten miles away – and the actual site chosen contained a pond and London's answer to the Eiffel Tower, Watkins' Folly.

5

This was to have been a tower taller than its French equivalent, and was named after the builder Edward Watkins, the Chairman of the Metropolitan Railway. That line carried grateful Londoners to the very spot at Wembley Park Station. Actually the tower had begun to tilt – shades of Pisa rather than Paris – and work was stopped at a very early stage; the remains were knocked down after World War I. The Exhibition itself came and went and its only epitaphs were the sad pavilions, later used as storehouses, on each side of the Olympic Way. But the stadium stayed and prospered, though it might have gone the way of the rest of the exhibition had not the Football Association expressed its interest.

The story of Wembley (and the name now means to the world the stadium and not the suburb) is a sad, vain, glorious gesture to the Empire which produced as its only lasting memorial the most famous sports venue in the world – the mecca of football. The idea of the Exhibition took firm shape in 1919. The King, the Prince of Wales, and Prime Minister Lloyd-George all gave it backing. But hardly anyone would give it money until the Prince of Wales, at the Imperial Conference of 1921, spoke of it as incorporating 'a great national sports ground' and announced that the FA were considering the stadium for the Cup Final.

Interest was instantly revived – even the citizens of Glasgow gave £105,000 to help build an attraction that would overshadow their own Hampden Park. While the stadium was the centrepiece, around it grew an astonishing collection of Exhibition buildings, each representing the architecture of the country of origin. The site was so vast that, despite ten million visitors a year, it lost a then astounding £5,000,000. Even the stadium was a financial failure. During the Exhibition it staged pageants, an international rodeo, and the Bristol pageant, an unlikely event reconstructing the history of that city.

The biggest event was the Empire Pageant, telling the history of the British Empire in three complete days. But though the crowds were adequate they were not vast, and even the first Cup Final only produced a revenue of £4714 as the stadium share of the gate. As a result, the whole Exhibition site was sold off for £300,000 in 1925 and contractors began to dismantle all but the stadium. The Palestine building became a Glasgow laundry, the West African furniture factory and a series of cafes were shipped to Bournemouth and reconstructed as the new grandstand for Bournemouth and Boscombe FC. There was even some doubt about the stadium itself until one of the contractors, Arthur Elvin, offered £122,500 for it – a down payment of £12,500 and ten one-year instalments.

It was a shrewd deal, for the stadium had actually cost somewhere in the region of £800,000 when it was completed well before the rest of the Exhibition in only 300 working days. To test the strength of the new structure, which contained 25,000 tons of concrete, 250,000 steel rivets, and 2000 tons of steel, a battalion of infantrymen were marched round and round the terracing.

The capacity was then regarded as 125,000 – a figure which was reduced by over 30,000 the following year – 23,000 of whom could be seated. This was over twice the attendance at the 1922 Cup Final at Stamford Bridge, and the Football Association felt quite confident about staging the 1923 event at Wembley – so confident that they felt there was no need to make the match, Bolton Wanderers against West Ham United, all ticket. But by lunchtime on April 28 1923, something like *four* times that maximum capacity was heading towards the new home of the Cup final!

Yet this was by no means the only game being played in London that day. At this time a full League programme was played on Cup Final day, for with no television or radio broadcasts, there was no competition to keep the fans away from their local grounds. A few miles east of Wembley, Arsenal were playing Sheffield United (the Gunners won 2–0); a few miles south Fulham were losing a Second Division home game against South Shields; and nearby Watford were entertaining Portsmouth in the Third Division South. Further south, Wolverhampton Wanderers crashed by five clear goals at Crystal Palace.

The most important game of the day, however, was still the Cup Final. But in fact it became very secondary to the sensational baptism of Wembley as a stage for prestigious football occasions. The contestants at an event where the players were to become barely relevant were First Division Bolton and West Ham, who had only entered the League in 1919, and were on the brink of promotion from Division Two (a 2–0 win at Hillsborough two days after the final was to clinch their place in Division One). Bolton, one of the founder members of the Football League, were just entering the most successful phase in their history, with three Cup wins and two third places in the League over seven seasons. The Hammers, though London's darlings that season, had no such immediate greatness to look forward to – it was to be 41 years before they were to win their first major honour and establish themselves amongst the leading clubs in the country and Europe.

But the fact that West Ham were playing in that first Wembley Cup final was one of the two major causes for the size of the crowd. The other was, of course, the new stadium itself, but it was not until around 1 pm that the authorities realised that the vast interest in the occasion was going to cause them serious trouble. By then it was too late. The stadium's own report on the event summed it up: 'The pressure was very great by 1pm. . . . By 1.45pm standing accommodation was nearly full and attempts were made to close the gates, and to inform the railway companies to stop all further trains.' But nothing stopped. The crowds kept on coming and, because of all the pre-publicity about the size of the new stadium, they had no reason to expect that they would not be able to get in.

'At 2pm,' says the report, 'Scotland Yard was asked for a large mounted force of police . . .' A case, if ever there was one, of the stable door being *opened* too late rather than closed too late! By 2.15 the crowd were battering impatiently on the exteriors of the new edifice and, undeterred, large numbers began to force an entry. The Official report states: 'The crowd broke through the barriers and it is estimated that another 100,000 got into the Stadium. The Board concludes that 150,000 got a good view of the match and the numbers may be estimated to have exceeded 200,000.' Some reports the following day put the figure as high as 250,000, making it easily the largest crowd

8

ever to have attended – they could not possibly have all watched – a football match.

All this pressure on the area around the ground created problems for the participants. The Bolton team coach was trapped in the traffic jam and the team (which had yet to win a major honour) had to prepare for this peak fixture by running the last mile to the ground. Once there they could not find a way inside which would not trap them in the middle of the crowd. They wandered around the perimeter fence and discovered a man digging a hole underneath it; he eventually widened it sufficiently to squeeze through and disappeared. The young men of Bolton sensibly followed.

The newspapers of the time provided scathing comments about the pandemonium and revealed incidents which have been clouded or forgotten since. The *Sunday Pictorial* commented: 'Nearly 1000 people were treated for injuries; there were 60 hospital cases and many broken bones. . . . The FA claim no responsibility for the arrangements, which were in the hands of the Stadium authorities.' Under a headline, 'Many Women Crushed', the *Pictorial* went on: 'Marvellous indeed that there was no fatality. Most of the injuries were the result of the stampeding crowd and a number of women were badly crushed against the railings. One man had to sit for two hours with a broken shoulder-blade because the Red Cross could not get through the crush. The King could see the various victims of the crush as they were being carried to the clearing station underneath the arches and above the royal box and it was noted that he displayed very great concern.'

The *Pictorial*'s reporter often appears more concerned with the King than with the crowd or with the match itself: 'Among all the pandemonium the King has never had a finer reception. Every hat was raised and there was a mighty sound as the great concourse sang "God Save the King", which was followed by three tremendous cheers. The King . . . made the excellent proposal that the officials should direct the crowd to pass below the arch beneath the royal stand and endeavour to take any seats that might be there. Thousands jumped at the chance and the entrance was soon blocked. . . .'

'It is certainly not too much to say that the tactful behaviour of the police,' continued the *Pictorial*, 'averted what might have been extremely ugly consequences. The crowd showed a very dangerous temper when it was suggested that the match might be impossible.'

Interestingly, neither the *Pictorial* nor any other of the following day's newspapers make any mention of the policeman on the white horse who played such a major part in controlling the crowds. This was a legend which clearly grew up later though many of the pictures of the masses show PC Scorey and Billy very clearly performing their now famous role.

One West Ham supporter, then only ten, recounted his own experiences thus: 'We arrived at one of the stations and joined the crowds. We were lucky. They were refusing to let some trains stop, which caused a lot of trouble. The crowd was so packed that we seemed to be literally carried along – for a long time my feet didn't even touch the ground! The stadium was up there in front. It was on a small hill, and to me at least it looked like the biggest building in the whole world.

'I don't remember there being any gates or turnstiles – we just reached a stairway. I suppose we must have come through a hole in a fence. We were literally kicked up the stairway. You couldn't turn back, you had to go on. When we got to the top there just wasn't anywhere to go. We had to walk over the heads of the people in front. In the end we found an empty seat. I don't know how. I hadn't even known we were in a seated rather than a standing area. I sat on my father's lap and we were lucky. When we arrived you couldn't see a blade of grass for the crowd, though in the end we did manage to see most of the game. It wasn't a very good match!'

With the crowd jammed so close to the touchline and the game continually interrupted, it was no wonder that neither side really played up to their known form. But it was a wonder that the game took place at all.

At 2.45 there seemed no chance that the match would start. The Irish and Grenadier Guards were like bad children – somewhere on the pitch they could be heard but not seen. Officials suggested to King George that he should leave. He declined and, at just that moment, a white horse called Billy and his rider, PC George Scorey, began to carve themselves a niche in football legend.

Said PC Scorey in a BBC interview afterwards: 'I'd never seen anything like Wembley that afternoon. As my horse picked his way onto the field I saw nothing but a sea of heads. There wasn't a blade of grass anywhere. Just as I thought it was impossible, I saw an opening near one of the goals. The horse was very good, easing them back with his nose and tail until we got a goal line cleared . . . they went back step by step and then sat down. It was mainly due to the horse. There were lots of other animals there, but perhaps because he was white he commanded more attention.'

The directors later stated their opinion that it was PC Scorey who had made it possible for the Final to proceed. He was not, in fact, a soccer fan and is reputed never to have attended another match, though the Wembley authorities often offered him tickets.

At 3.44pm, nearly three-quarters of an hour late, the game began. At 3.46 David Jack – later to become the first player to command a £10,000 fee – scored Wembley's very first goal. Seddon intercepted a West Ham clearance, passed to Jack, and the Bolton player shot so hard that Hufton in the Hammers goal stood no chance. Neither did the supporters behind the goal, whom the ball knocked down as though they were dominoes. At the time West Ham right-half Tresadern, who had just taken a throw-in, was trapped in the crowd.

The half lasted for over an hour, the game being stopped every so often to get spectators off the pitch. The players were unable to get back to the dressing room, so they just changed ends and got straight on with the game. Bolton started the second half just as they had the first. After just seven minutes, Ted Vizard roared down the left-wing, and centred to John Smith, who volleyed onto the underside of the bar only to see the ball hit the ground and bounce straight out. But the goal was given – a remarkably controversial goal for such an unlikely setting – and the referee hesitated only briefly. A similar event was to occur, of course, in the 1966 World Cup Final at the same end. Smith's goal has since been celebrated because of the story that the ball was kept in play by a spectator who struck his foot over the line and passed to Vizard. The winger admitted that this did happen during the match, but not on that particular run. The tale, lost in the mists of time, persists.

After the second goal the game was effectively over. Went a contemporary report: 'From then on to the last whistle the game was as interesting as a Cup Final is generally expected to be.' Bolton had won the Cup for the first time, and their supporters could still be found in the Stadium at 7pm celebrating the fact. Probably because they could not find a way out through the thronging concourse! The FA declared that the result would stand and counted the takings – £27,776 – easily the highest ever taken at a single sporting event, though £2797 had to be returned to supporters who claimed not to be able to reach their seats, or if they did found them occupied by others.

PC Scorey returned home to tell his fiancée that his day had been 'just ordinary'. Not everyone was as pleased with the mounted police as the Board of the Stadium. West Ham relied on their fast running wingers – Richards and Ruffell – and their trainer, Charlie Paynter, complained afterwards: 'It was hopeless. Our wingers kept tumbling all over the place, tripping in great ruts, hoof marks and holes.' Sadly for Paynter, those same holes had not seemed to upset Bolton's flying winger Ted Vizard.

The main memories, inevitably, were of the crowd. Stories of men climbing up the drainpipes to the roof were legion and true. Many people got into the ground by either climbing over the gates or simply being carried through holes where turnstiles used to be. One old man was observed literally demolishing the wooden fencing with a hatchet, getting through and then being kicked up the stairs by the crowd behind. It was an unprecedented scene and it never happened again. The following year the FA made the Cup Final all-ticket, and it has remained that way ever since. And Wembley Stadium, for all its frightening baptism, has become the undisputed home of the premier occasion in domestic football.

DIXIE DEAN - GOAL MACHINE

The goalscoring record that may never be beaten

In June 1926 death stared into the face of William Ralph Dean, a 19-year-old centre-forward with First Division Everton. He was not expected to survive after sickeningly crashing his motor-cycle in the North Wales village of Holywell. A broken jaw and damaged legs were his lesser wounds; his life hung on a thread because of a fractured skull.

Dean, known from childhood as 'Dixie' (a nickname he abhorred), because of his tanned complexion and black hair, had just completed the best season of his football career. He had crossed the Mersey from his home-town team, Tranmere Rovers, to join Everton in 1925, and after an impressive debut against Arsenal at Highbury in March of that year, his prolific scoring feats in the Central League had earned him a regular first-team place.

In the 1925–26 season he had scored 32 First Division goals, many of them with deft flicks from that dark head, which suffered such terrible damage as he was flung from his motorbike. The message to the Everton officials from the hospital in North Wales was transparently clear: if Dean came through major surgery he would never head a football again.

His sheer natural strength, coupled with the surgeon's artistry, cheated death and while the Everton management began planning for a new centre-forward, Dean was transferred to a nursing home in the West Derby suburb of Liverpool. Again, from his convalescence, the official message was emphatic – he would never be able to play again. Strips of steel had been integral in the repair of his skull and there they would

13

have to remain; in 1926 no man could participate in such a physical sport under that handicap.

His doctors happily pronounced that there had been no brain damage, but began to doubt their own verdict when Dean announced that he was reporting back to Everton as a player! Still in pain from his knee injuries he limped out of the nursing home and into the care of the club trainer, Harry Cooke.

Within days he was heading a tennis ball, and under the attentive guidance of Cooke the scars, the bruises, and the headaches were all overcome. Four months after he had been fighting for his life he was battling again for goals. A further four months later his fitness was so unquestioned and his form so outstanding that he was chosen for the first time for England, against Wales at Wrexham, scoring twice in a 3–3 draw.

It was a recovery that captured the imagination of the foot-balling public. 'Dixie' Dean became their superman, an idol capable of extraordinary achievements; still not 21 he super-seded all his contemporaries in popularity. And if most of the country simply admired and wholly respected the bravery and the talent of the youngster from Birkenhead, on Merseyside he was loved with a passion rarely witnessed outside Liverpool.

But Dean did not milk the sympathetic response with which his return to the game was greeted; he did not want to be remembered just as a player who had proved that medical science made no allowance for will and spirit. He created new memories.

His England career had a remarkable start. He followed up his two-goal debut at Wrexham by claiming both England goals in a surprise 2–1 win over Scotland at Hampden Park – the winner coming from a solo run of devastating power which reinforced the claim that he was not simply a great header of the ball. Five weeks later he scored a hat-trick in a 9–1 win over Belgium, and then another three goals in the 5–2 beating of Luxembourg. He brought his total to 12 goals in his first five internationals with another double in a 6–0 victory over France in Paris.

His 21 League goals, after missing the start of that season had kept Everton in the First Division, along with a cheque-book philosophy which still applied to the club nearly 50 years later. Warney Cresswell, the England full-back, cost £7000 from Sunderland, a staggering price for the times, and was one of several expensive purchases who helped Everton finish third from bottom and avoid relegation.

Dean would have been the first to admit that a change in the rules had created a profitable era for goalscorers. Astute defenders in the early 1920s had formulated a highly effective offside trap which had dramatically reduced the number of goals scored. The Irish full-back Billy McCracken of Newcastle United had laid out the blueprint for the plan so accurately that visiting players alighting from their train at Newcastle Station would hear a guard's whistle and proclaim 'Oh no, surely we're not offside already!'

In 1925 the Football Association acted to reduce the number of defenders needed to play an attacker onside from three to two, and thereby ruined McCracken's master plan. In the First Division alone goals rose by 40 per cent, and some extravagant scoring performances were recorded. Perhaps the most startling was a new League scoring record, coming in the 1925–27 season, from George Camsell – the Middlesbrough forward who could have been bought for £50 at the time of Dean's accident. He scored 59 League goals as his club won the Second Division Championship, and 75 in all matches.

But though much was expected of Dean as he trained for the 1927–28 season – a little more than a year after his accident – the most fervent Evertonian could not have hoped for the excitement that was to be drawn out until the very last breath of the new campaign.

Dean's reputation by now ensured him of diligent and often furious attention from opponents. But contrary to expectation, Everton made a creditable start, cast in the image of anything but a side which had scrambled to safety the year before. Cresswell brought stability to the backs; a Scot from Airdrie, Hunter Hart, developed into an outstanding attacking centre-half, while outside-left Alec Troup provided Dean's service.

The official Everton club history of the time unflatteringly describes Troup as 'a grim little player', but the winger, who stood no more than 5ft 6in., was a craftsman at crossing the ball, and few centre-halves could deny the leaping Dean in the air.

At the start of October, Everton were seventh in the table, and in that month their form became expansive. On October 8, Dean scored all five goals in a 5-2 win over Manchester United; on the 22nd Everton destroyed West Ham by seven clear goals; and on the 29th they won 3-1 at Portsmouth to top the League. By way of celebration they devastated Leicester 7-1 on the first Saturday of November.

They led through December and January as Dean's goals ticked up with the regularity of the fare on a taxi-driver's meter. But in February they faltered when they visited their closest rivals Huddersfield Town, the champions of 1924, 1925, and 1926 and runners-up in 1927. Everton lost 4-1 in Huddersfield and they did not win again for seven matches.

They were beaten 5-2 at home by Tottenham Hotspur; they drew 3-3 in the derby game at Anfield; and then failed to score in their next four matches – a run which yielded just one point. Another point came in a 2-2 home draw with Derby County, before they won 2-0 at Sunderland on March 31 – without Dean, who was spending his time less profitably that afternoon leading England's attack without distinction against Scotland at Wembley; they lost 5-1 to the team which became known as the Wembley Wizards.

Their win at Roker Park put Everton three points behind Huddersfield, and the Yorkshire club, who had also reached the FA Cup Final, were strongly fancied to win the first 'double' of the 20th century. But while Dean and Everton found strength for the last stretch, Huddersfield faltered.

The final in 1928 was played before the League season ended, on April 21, so that up to that match the Huddersfield players performed with one eye on Wembley, and after they had lost there, 3-1 to Blackburn Rovers, they became demoralised.

Everton, with Dean continually devastating in front of goal, were not to lose another League match following their defeat of

Sunderland, and as Dean's goal count moved well into the 40s the club now had their targets – the League title and Camsell's record.

The championship became the easier proposition. On the morning of the penultimate Saturday of the season Everton, with two games left to play, led the League with 50 points; Huddersfield, with four games remaining, totalled 47. Dean had extended his goalscoring tally to 53, but he needed an improbable seven from just three hours of football to set a new standard.

On that Saturday Huddersfield won 2–1 at Leicester to keep alive their title hopes, while Everton, needing to win but also hoping for the goals to fall Dean's way, travelled to Turf Moor.

Burnley were struggling at the foot of the table, but in their captain, Jack Hill, they possessed one of the most effective centre-halves in the League. Hill had played for England in several of Dean's internationals; a tall man, he was favoured to compete well against the Everton star in the air and he had earned his England opportunities by a reputation as a tight, tenacious marker. To the supporters who made the short journey from Liverpool to Turf Moor, Dean must have seemed a long way from the record. Camsell, who had been scoring almost as consistently in the First Division during this season as he had in the past year in the second, must have believed that his target would not be reached.

But for Dean, Hill was no mountain. Everton took away the two points they wanted to keep Huddersfield at bay, winning by five goals to three. Four of those goals were credited to 'Dixie' Dean, taking his total to 57; so from the remaining fixture against Arsenal at Goodison Park he needed two to equal Camsell's record and a hat-trick to break it.

Had Everton also needed to beat Arsenal to win the Championship, the occasion might have been too much for even the impassioned Evertonian sense of drama. But in the week leading up to the match Huddersfield had to play twice, and in post-Wembley depression they lost at home to Sheffield United and away to Aston Villa – refuting those who argue that fixture congestion is an exclusive product of the 1960s and 1970s. By these two Huddersfield defaults Everton, 20th the previous season, became the 1927–28 champions.

More than 60,000 crammed Goodison for the Arsenal match to greet the new champions; now their cause was unilateral – win or lose Dean had to get a hat-trick. Before the kick-off Mr. J. McKenna, the League President, presented the trophy to Warney Cresswell, who had the unusual facility, for the times, of being able to thank his supporters over a public address system.

The ceremonials heightened the sense of occasion. And as the players warmed-up on a pleasant May afternoon all eyes turned towards Dean, the crowd all conjecture. But it was Arsenal who scored first, a goal presented to them by Everton defenders who seemed totally intent on creating for their own centre-forward rather than frustrating the opposition. An Arsenal forward was allowed to turn and shoot, though the poorly struck effort rolled straight at Arthur Davies. The Everton goalkeeper reacted casually and the ball brushed past his hands, slid on through his legs and came gently to rest against the back of the net.

Slightly abashed, Everton drove forward on to the attack, with each player searching selflessly to create a chance for Dean. And the terraces, baying hungrily, didn't have to wait long for the first course. Dean moved magnetically towards any ball in the penalty area and then suddenly his instinct for goal carried him above a defender and he guided in a header for the equaliser – his 58th goal was also Everton's hundredth of the League season – the only club to be so prolific.

Arsenal, in the middle of the table, had only their personal pride to sustain their efforts, but the furore from the packed ground provided inspiration. If Dean was to break the record, he was to receive no assistance from the opposition. But though Arsenal kept Everton at full stretch, they could not prevent Dean from acquiring a second goal.

Everton were awarded a penalty, which Dean would have been delegated to take whether records were in the air or not. The audience ran the gamut of emotions – the roar of delight at the decision, the buzz of anticipation as he placed the ball, the hush of tension as he began his run and the full-throated shouts of delight as he placed his shot firmly into the net. Incredibly he had equalled the record and his 59 goals had been scored against First Division defences, unlike Camsell's.

As though they were totally aware of the proximity of history, the Everton team began to stumble and fumble, and for the second time they presented Arsenal with a goal. Davies was again at fault as he and left-back O'Donnell misread each other's intentions as they moved towards a loose ball on the edge of their own penalty area. O'Donnell's attempt at a back-pass only succeeded in him steering it past his confused goal-keeper, and the North London side were, to their own surprise, back on terms.

It mattered little to anyone in the ground, except that it stole valuable time for Dean's quest for his 60th goal. No amount of stage managing could have fashioned such excitement as the second-half melted like an ice cube in the sun. The minutes raced by. Dean continued to stalk the environs of the Arsenal goal, but neither on his own nor with the assistance of those around him could he etch an opening. And unlike Everton, Arsenal were in no mood to distribute gifts.

But Dean at last found his most formidable ally in Alec Troup, the diminutive Scottish winger, the only man to play in all 42 games of Everton's League season (Dean played in 39), and the only player apart from Dean to reach double figures in goals – Troup had scored ten.

Yet Troup's main value to the side had been in his work with Dean, the precision with which he fed crosses to the centre-forward. Now with just over five minutes remaining Troup hung another tempting centre over the Arsenal goalmouth. Dean, sensing that this might be his last chance, timed his approach to perfection and hammered his header over the line.

With just moments of his season remaining 'Dixie' Dean had broken the record, and appropriately he scored his 60th goal in his definitive style – the unstoppable header. He was teaching the game about aerial artistry.

His team-mates rushed to his side and swamped him with congratulations in the style of the day – back-slapping and hand-shakes rather than kissing and cuddling! Dean, a humourous, outwardgoing, but genuinely modest man, reacted with a smile and kept his famous head bowed as though faintly embarrassed at the fuss he had caused. He was certainly surprised when one fan sprinted onto the pitch to shake his hand, followed by a second who planted a large kiss on his cheek. The referee seized the second intruder by the scruff of the neck and threw him to the ground. In 1928 such a pitch invasion was almost as sensational as Dean's achievement itself.

No one minded when Arsenal, who had more than played their part in the proceedings, equalised again, this time with a good goal, in the very last minute. And though Huddersfield won their last match the same afternoon, Everton had finished champions by two clear points.

The players dined that night with the directors, and Dean characteristically played down his feat in a speech to the assembled company, thanking his colleagues for all their help and singling out Alec Troup for special praise. Further celebrations included nights out at the Empire Theatre on the Monday and the Shakespeare the following evening and on the next day Everton left on a tour of Switzerland.

Dean had not finished his season for he was invited to represent England against Belgium and France, his scoring touch still sure as he netted twice in each international. His final tally of 82 senior goals included three in the FA cup and 19 in representative football; he scored five goals in a match on two occasions, four goals twice, six hat-tricks and two goals in 17 different matches – all this less than two years after his life, let alone his football career, had hung in the balance.

He continued to score goals for Everton until 1938, almost coming within reach of his own record with 45 League goals in 1931–32. His buoyant personality sustained him even though he was often battered black and blue from the attentions of frustrated defenders. And when Everton bought Tommy

Lawton to succeed him he passed on his skills with a warmth and generosity that the youngster never forgot.

Perhaps he was sure in his mind that whatever Lawton would achieve, he would never come near that record 60 League goals – just as no forward has done since.

THE WEMBLEY WIZARDS

The story of Scotland's greatest victory at Wembley

Viewed unemotionally, the history of Scottish football can be summed up in the records of three very great clubs (Queens Park, Rangers, and Celtic) and a century of matches against the enemy south of the border. For most of its history, and perhaps even now, the main objective of Scottish football has been to defeat England – and in that objective the Scots have succeeded more often than they have failed. At the end of 1976 the tally stood at 37 Scottish victories to England's 35, with 22 matches drawn.

But among all these matches one stands out and, nearly 50 years later, will regularly provoke eulogies in Glasgow pubs – the Wembley Wizards game of 1928. It is still used as the ultimate proof that the Scots play football better than the English or, indeed, anyone else. All the odder then, that when the Scots team was announced it was greeted with a burst of criticism rarely equalled before or since.

It was the forward line, later to be quickly lionized and then immortalized, which drew most of the initial criticism. The names that now ring magically – Alex Jackson, Jimmy Dunn, Hughie Gallacher, Alex James, and Alan Morton – were then seen as a bunch of midgets, none being over 5ft 7in, likely to be eaten by the giant England defence. Hughie Gallacher, who had not played for more than two months, was preferred to Celtic's Jimmy McGrory. It was to be Scotland's sad misfortune that the playing careers of probably the best two centre-forwards she has ever produced should coincide.

Gallacher was ultimately a tragic figure. He married too early, was divorced after an unhappy few years during which a son died in infancy, was hardly a total abstainer (after a tour of Hungary he was the subject of an inquiry, being accused and acquitted of being drunk and disorderly on the field) and, ultimately, in 1957, had to face a charge of ill-treating his daughter.

He never reached the court; on the night of June 11 1957 a lone figure was seen deliberately walking in front of an express near his home in Gateshead. His 387 goals in 541 Laegue matches and 22 goals for Scotland mattered little then. But back in the 1920s Gallacher was without a peer. In the first half of the decade he played for Airdrieonians, being the major reason for their four consecutive second places in the League (they never won the trophy) and their sole Scottish Cup success of 1924. In one memorable spell he scored 30 goals in 5 matches, but he was just as adept at making them as at scoring them.

As ever, money talked in the end and he went to Newcastle for £6500 in 1925. There he was a hero, despite his unathletic 5ft 5in physique. He stayed five years, during which he was made captain and led United to the Championship, and then cost Chelsea £10,000. But the decline was about to start a rapidly accelerating trail leading through Derby County, Notts County, Grimsby, and finally Gateshead.

Far happier was Alan Morton, a winger the Scots still rate higher than Matthews or Finney and the only player invited to the Scottish FA diamond jubilee dinner in 1933. He played against England 12 times between 1920 and 1932 and not once did they subdue him. His ball control, balance, and sheer dribbling artistry put him in a class of his own. Born one of five sons of a miner in Jordanhill, Glasgow, he practised throughout his childhood up against the walls and doors of that typically terraced part of Scotland, as well as with his brothers, who formed half a useful team in later life.

Alan followed one of those brothers, Bob, to Queen's Park. In his first game, against Third Lanark, he calmly dribbled round Scotland's goalkeeper Jimmy Brownlie for a cheeky goal. In 1920, the year of his first game against England when he scored with a lob from the touchline, Morton moved to

Rangers as the only semi-professional in Willie Struth's very professional outfit. And, although he was easily the highest paid player in Britain at that time, he continued with his career as a mining engineer, usually working on the morning of matches, even Home Internationals, and going straight to Ibrox or Hampden from his office. The 1920s were Rangers' greatest period, and Alan Morton was their brightest star. He would have few rivals, if any, for the title of Scotland's greatest forward.

Among Morton's few serious rivals for that title is surely Alex James, the man around whom Herbert Chapman built the great Arsenal side of the 1930s. Like Gallacher he moved south in 1925, from Raith Rovers to Second Division Preston. At Deepdale he entertained and developed his reputation for impish and bewildering tricks. It is unlikely that James took Second Division football very seriously; he enjoyed the game there rather more than he did after Chapman paid a surprisingly small £8750 for him in 1929. James was the key for Arsenal, but he had to be regimented. At Highbury, the game was about winning and James played back, developing his famous pass inside the back to the wingers, Bastin and Hulme, as well as the sharp bursts out of trouble in midfield. In 1928 he was at his most adventurous and inventive, coming forward for long speculative shots and performing every imaginable trick in midfield. On his day, it is unlikely that any provider in Britain could have compared.

It was the custom of the time to announce the team outside the office of the Scottish FA in Carleton Place, inevitably bringing the traffic to a halt for an hour before and afterwards. The crowd there on March 21 – ten days before the match – was as uniformly scathing as the newspapers. There was no Meiklejohn, McPhail, or McGrory, but there were eight Anglos (Scots playing for English clubs) – an immediate source of criticism. Said the *Daily Record*: 'It's not a great team.'

The players disagreed. England were not playing well that season, either – despite having the likes of Dixie Dean, Roy Goodall, and West Ham's Ted Hufton in goal. They had been beaten by both Ireland and Wales, scoring but one goal, and this was to be the only season in the history of the Home International Championship that England lost all her three games. The Scots had done little better, drawing with Wales and losing to Ireland at Hampden. That explained the 'new look' team, which was well aware that the losers of the forthcoming game would finish bottom of the Home Championship table (a rather more significant matter than it is today).

The Scots team contained only three Scottish League players – Harkness, Dunn, and Morton. They travelled South with 11 trainloads of supporters, each paying an excursion fare of 25s 6d (£1.27). The team met on the Friday night in the chaos of Piccadilly, where they were staying at the Regent Palace Hotel. It was not an inspired venue – Alex Jackson disappeared for the night and Alex James (in his more subtle way) kept the Scottish trainer Jimmy Kerr up by starting a rumour that he had gone out on the town, and then sleeping in another room.

But it was at the Regent Palace where one of the great legends of Scottish football was enacted. Jimmy McMullan the captain, was asked to give the team a tactical talk. He is reputed to have said, simply: 'The President wants us to discuss football, but you all know what's expected of you. All I've got to say is, go to bed and pray for rain.' It worked, and as an added bonus, England's captain, Bishop, was taken ill during the night and had to withdraw.

By the time the teams reached Wembley there was a downpour, giving the Scots forwards a tremendous advantage over the bulky English defenders. In the dressing room the Scots remained confident – amused by Alex James sending out for a baggier pair of shorts to maintain his well-publicized image.

The less than capacity 80,868 fans could not have enjoyed the pouring rain, and waited silently for the teams to be presented to the Duke of York (later King George VI) and, rather less likely, King Amanullah of Afghanistan.

Within minutes Scotland had scored. Huddersfield winger Smith saw his and England's first shot hit the post and rebound to McMullan, who passed quickly on to James and then Morton. The great winger took it to the line and crossed for Alec Jackson to head home.

The rest of the half was reasonably even, with Harkness keeping the England forwards at bay on several occasions with good saves and half-backs McMullan and Jimmy Gibson gradually acquiring control of the muddy middle of the field. A minute before half-time James got the ball again, beat Wilson, Healless, and Jones in a memorable run, and then shot from the edge of the penalty area. The ball evaded Hufton and Scotland were in the unexpected position of being two up as they trooped off for the interval.

In the second half Scotland really took control. James hit the bar, then Jackson scored a replica of the first goal from another Morton cross. James added a fourth immediately afterwards. With just five minutes left Jackson completed a remarkable hat-trick – remarkable in that yet again it was a header from a Morton cross scored by a member of Scotland's smallest-ever forward line.

In the final minute England scored with a 40-yard free-kick from Bob Kelly, but only served to emphasise how completely they had been outplayed. The Scots were euphoric. The newspapers took back all their criticism. Said the *Glasgow Herald:* 'The success of the Scots was primarily another demonstration that Scottish skill, science, and trickery will prevail against the less attractive and simpler methods of the English style . . .' Something of an exaggeration perhaps. The English selectors were blamed for choosing six of the players who were to appear in the following week's Blackburn-Huddersfield Cup Final – but it had hardly affected Huddersfield's Jackson.

England, it must be remembered, had been having a poor season anyway, but they were thoroughly exposed by a forward line unusually well suited to the conditions. While they concentrated (unsuccessfully) on marking the wingers, Jackson and Morton, inside-forwards James and Jimmy Dunn (the Hibs forward who was to join Everton and score in the 1933 Cup Final) and the great centre-forward Hughie

Gallacher were able to weave patterns all over the England half, in a fashion they could hardly have predicted.

None the less it was a freak result. Basically a very poor England side, a fortunate blend on the day of virtually randomly selected Scots forwards, and conditions which unusually handicapped one team and benefitted the other, had combined to produce a result which proved little of lasting significance except confirmation of the length of Scottish memories.

At Hampden the following year the Scots carried on the good work with a rather more pedestrian 1–0 win, though it did enable them to take the Championship for the seventh time in a decade. But there was no more wizardry and there has not been a performance to match that of 1928 since. But the Scots still hope . . .

WALSALL 2, ARSENAL O

One of the most remarkable score-lines of all time

The 1930s were dominated by one club in a way that no decade had been before or has been since. That club was Arsenal. They won the League in 1931, 1933, 1934, 1935, and 1938, the Cup in 1930 and 1936, and were runners up twice in each competition. And yet, if most football fans were asked to name a single game played by Arsenal in the 1930s, then nine times out of ten they would recall one of two games that Arsenal lost – the 1932 Cup Final against Newcastle, with football's most disputed goal, or the third round tie that ended Walsall 2 Arsenal 0 on January 14 1933.

The latter must still rank as the greatest giant-killing feat of all time, despite the fact that Walsall were high in the Third Division and Arsenal were playing away. Four decades later it is certainly possible to argue that Wimbledon's defeat of Burnley – the only time since the formation of the Third Division that a non-League club has won on a First Division ground – Hereford's victory over Newcastle or Yeovil's humiliation of Sunderland should rank higher. And yet the emotions always return to Walsall and Arsenal, and the reasons why have little to do with the Midland club but much to do with the Gunners.

In the 1930s Arsenal meant football and football meant Arsenal. It was because of that decade that they probably remain the most famous football club in the world today – challenged only by Real Madrid and Manchester United. On one famous occasion they provided seven of the England team that took on and defeated the new world champions, Italy. The game, appropriately, was played at Highbury.

Arsenal were always the team to beat. After the local club, everyone looked first for the Arsenal result on a Saturday night.

The Gunners probably reached the peak of their abilities on December 24 1932, crushing Sheffield United 8–2 in a devastating display with goals from Lambert (4), Bastin (2), Hulme, and Jack. They achieved more trophies after that game than before it, but it was the pinnacle of their potential, the moment when they firmly staked their claim as the team of the 1930s. Just three weeks later, Arsenal were due to play their first FA Cup match of the season at the Fellows Park home of Walsall, a Third Division North club of few pretensions and even less history. The scene barely seemed set for a game that was still to be recalled with reverence nearly half a century later.

One comparison sums up this meeting of David and Goliath – Arsenal had spent more that season on new boots than Walsall had paid for their entire team. Of such limited material is history made.

The Gunners were London's first professional club, entering the League as far back as 1893 and sneaking into the First Division by less than fair means in 1919, having finished only sixth in the Second Division in the immediate pre-War season. Nevertheless, someone's faith was well founded for they have not left Division One since. They remained a middling club until the traumatic year of 1925, when Herbert Chapman left Huddersfield half way through the first ever hat-trick of Championships to join Arsenal. He was to lead Arsenal to the same feat and his two clubs remain the only ones ever to have completed this hat-trick.

It is indicative of Chapman's reputation that, when Arsenal appoint a new manager – and they periodically do – the press invariably print the same picture. It consists of the aspirant standing before the bust of the great man in the main hall at Highbury. And the captions always ask the same question, 'Have the Gunners found an equal?' The answer, one supposes, must always be no. For no one will ever again have the scope that Chapman had, nor the social conditions so conducive to his kind of autocracy, nor, perhaps, his insight into the way to win football matches.

On the field of play the system that Chapman devised became the norm for 30 years. And it was not only on the park that Chapman showed football the future. In Tom Whittaker he found and encouraged the first of the genuine physiotherapists. In Highbury he built the best club ground in Britain. In advocating floodlights, numbered shirts, white balls ('a stunt' declared the FA), goal judges, independent time-keepers (he installed a 45-minute clock at Highbury only to have it banned by the FA), savings schemes for the players, and even supporters' trains he was way ahead of his time. He was, in fact, the first professional in a world of amateurs.

But what was perhaps his greatest off-field achievement is still visible to the millions who travel by London's Piccadilly Line. There, sandwiched between Finsbury Park and Holloway Road, is Arsenal underground station. Not Gillespie Road, as the London Transport Passenger Board had originally called the stop, nor Highbury Hill, a compromise suggestion later put forward, but plain, unadorned Arsenal. Chelsea are on the doorstep of Fulham Broadway Station, West Ham next door to Upton Park – what more needs to be said about the powers of persuasion of this remarkable man?

In fact his success was all the more spectacular following, as it did, a totally undistinguished playing career. The only memorable thing about his years as a Spurs reserve (Arsenal being their arch-rivals probably influenced his decision to move) is often said to be his lemon-coloured boots.

Chapman joined Arsenal for a variety of reasons. He knew that Huddersfield would never be a truly great club. The town was too small, too remote, too devoted to the rival Rugby League. With Arsenal he had the largest city in the world on his doorstep, with a ground less than half an hour from Piccadilly Circus. And, as London had yet to greet a League Championship, the timing of his move was auspicious, for 1925 was the year that saw a footballing revolution. The 'offside' game had produced such a decline in goalscoring that the International Board changed the law from 'three defenders between attacker and goal . . .' to 'two defenders . . .'. The immediate result was a glut of goals, and it was Chapman who eventually perfected the defensive solution, although there is considerable evidence to suggest that he did not actually originate it.

One of Chapman's first buys was Charlie Buchan from Sunderland, for £2,000 down and £100 for every goal he scored that season. Buchan's return to Arsenal, the club he had actually walked out on before the War over 11 shillings expenses, was not a very happy one. One of his, and Chapman's, earliest matches for the club was a humiliating 7–0 defeat at Newcastle on October 6 1925. Buchan was so upset at such a return to the North-east that he and Chapman organized an immediate tactical discussion. One or the other (accounts vary as to who it was) proposed that Arsenal's centre-half, Jack Butler, should adopt a purely defensive role and that one of the inside-forwards should drop back to supply the creative link between defence and attack that the centre-half could no longer provide.

Oddly enough Newcastle's centre-half, Charlie Spencer, claimed he had played just such a defensive role in that vital match, and the Arsenal plan may have come from observing Newcastle's success. Before 1925 the centre-half performed exactly the functions his title implied – he had played in the middle of the field, helping in defence and instigating attacks.

Buchan expected to be given the creative inside-forward's job himself, but Chapman valued his goalscoring abilities too highly, and detailed a reserve inside-forward, Andy Neil, to perform the midfield role at Upton Park the following week on Monday, October 8 1925. Arsenal won 4–0, with Buchan scoring twice.

Chapman gradually revised his team by pushing the full-backs out to mark the wingers, and using both his wing-halves (now free of their close-marking duties) to perform the midfield duties along with the withdrawn inside-forward. The scheme worked well enough, but was not perfected until Chapman purchased the vital creative link, Alex James, from Preston in 1929. Thus the team played in a formation which could loosely be described as 3-4-3 or 3-3-4, rather than the 2-3-5 of the pre-World War I era. He also purchased scoring wingers in Cliff Bastin and Joe Hulme to make use of Alex James's (the ultimate mid-field link) long passes.

Within a season at Arsenal, Chapman had created the third-back game in response to the new offside law and torn Chairman Henry Norris's no-transfer policy to shreds (the advert Arsenal had placed in the Athletic News had said 'anyone who considers paying exorbitant transfer fees should not bother to apply'). And at the end of that time Arsenal were runners-up to Huddersfield in the League. It was the highest a London club had ever finished. The great days had begun.

The following year Arsenal were at Wembley – as they were again in 1930. The latter was the first year the teams ran out together and subsequently shared the same reception – a mark of respect for Chapman, as the two clubs involved were Huddersfield and Arsenal. The Gunners won 2-0; they were just on the verge of greatness. For Huddersfield it was the final gesture of a glorious decade – they would never win anything again.

But down at Highbury, Chapman was going from strength to strength. With Arsenal taking the Championships of 1931 and 1933, returning to Wembley for the notorious over-the-line final of 1932 and continuing to build at a time when the country was going from crisis to crisis, and many clubs were being forced close to bankruptcy. They were already being talked about as a phenomenon more remarkable than the two-or-three season wonders that usually provide football's winners.

The names of the men Chapman found or taught are testimony in themselves – Hulme, Roberts, Hapgood, Lambert, Parker, John, Copping, Moss, Male – and when he had to buy he rarely made a mistake – Charles Buchan, David Jack (the first five-figure footballer), Cliff Bastin, and Alex James, to name only the best known of his acquisitions.

At Arsenal he was able to buy more freely than at Huddersfield. When he needed the vital link for his carefully developed 3-4-3 system in 1929 he was able to spend the then enormous sum of £9000 on Alex James. But equally he was adept at finding the right men from more obscure habitats. Herbie Roberts, the perfect 'stopper' centre-half, came from Oswestry for a mere £200, Cliff Bastin was purchased for £2000 from Exeter after he had played only 17 League games for the Third Division side and ultimately proved Chapman's hunch by scoring 33 goals in 1932-33 – the highest total ever by a conventional winger in a League season.

That same season, Arsenal were already half a dozen points clear when they arrived at Fellows Park on that fateful day. Not that Chapman was at his happiest. He had several first team men out of action. England left-back and club captain Eddie Hapgood was injured, left-half Bob John and the two centre-forwards (Jack Lambert and Tim Coleman) all had flu, England winger Joe Hulme was off form and had been dropped. Chapman decided to risk none of them and brought in four unknowns – Norman Sidey, Tommy Black, Billy Warnes, and Charlie Walsh. Only Sidey had played for the first team before. As it happened, he was the only one to do so again.

Chapman has been accused of underestimating the opposition. This seems unlikely. He had carefully checked out Walsall, a club that was to apply for re-election a record seven times while shuttling between the North and South sections of the Third Division. They had drawn three of their previous four matches and lost the other 5-0. One newspaper was quite carried away by the differences between these Lords and serfs of the English League: 'Arsenal the rich, the confident, the League leaders, the £30,000 aristocrats, against the little Midland Third Division team that cost £69 in all when Arsenal own £87 worth of boots . . .'

Chapman was very probably not lulled – he may have gambled that his reserves would react to the challenge just as the Walsall team was bound to, fighting all the way. And, after all, he still had the likes of George Male, Herbie Roberts, David Jack, Alex James, and Cliff Bastin. Of the game, there is not terribly much to say, as tends to be the case on these occasions. Arsenal were strangely nervous – Walsh had put his boots on in the dressing room without noticing that he was not wearing stockings – and Walsall's violent tackling, particularly on James, confirmed all expectations. None the less, the Walsall back line of Bennett, Bird, and Leslie were magnificent in absorbing all that the Gunners could throw at them. Even when good chances did fall their way, Arsenal contrived to make a mess of them (Walsh caught the best centre of the first half with his shoulder rather than his head).

After an hour the Londoners were beginning to breath a little more easily; no score and, seemingly at worst, the prospect of a Highbury replay ahead. Then it happened. Lee sent across a corner and Gilbert Alsop, Walsall's centre-forward, headed home. Forty-two years later, in 1975, Alsop was still connected with the club, as groundsman, when Walsall produced their next giant-killing run with Cup defeats of both Manchester United and Newcastle United.

Chapman ordered that Jack should lead the attack. It paid off almost immediately as Jack shaped to score, only for the wretched Walsh to take the ball off him. Five minutes later another of the newcomers, Black, who had been getting increasingly irritated with both Walsall's tactics and Arsenal's inability to cope with them, sealed his side's fate by bringing Alsop down in the area. Sheppard scored from the spot and the game was over.

Chapman reacted, probably over-reacted, violently to the defeat – the worst humiliation of his whole managerial career. Of the newcomers, only Sidey remained beyond the end of the season. So angry was Chapman with Black that the very same night he declared Black would never play for Arsenal again, and, according to some stories, refused to even allow him to come near Highbury until his transfer to Plymouth the following week. Perhaps the name Black, summoning up visions of black days in the Black Country, was too much for Chapman. Walsh moved to Brentford within a fortnight, and Warnes went to Norwich in May.

The result did not affect Arsenal's League form, and they won the Championship by four points from Aston Villa, going on to a hat-trick that has not been repeated by any team since. Walsall were knocked out 2–0 by eventual finalists

Manchester City in the next round, but finished a respectable fifth in the Third Division North that season.

The game, then, was not particularly remarkable. The result has certainly been equalled and probably bettered by clubs less revered than Walsall. For the game's real significance we must put it in its historical perspective.

The 1930s were, for most of provincial Britain, the worst decade of a miserable half-century. In many of the textile towns of the North, unemployment came to a third of the work-force. In some coal-mining and ship-building towns, like Jarrow, or the valleys of South Wales, a whole society was on the dole for literally years on end. To these towns came Arsenal, representing the wealth, the affluence and the unfair advantage that London appeared to have stolen from the rest of the country, and more particularly, that part of the country which had long produced Britain's wealth.

It was not so unrealistic to see Arsenal – London's first Champions – as a symbol of the wealth earned in the North, but spent and enjoyed in London. With the local football ground being one of the few entertainment outlets available to the vast majority of the population (and certainly the most emotionally significant with its overtones of local pride and strident masculinity), it is not surprising that Arsenal became the subject of fierce emotional commitment – one way or the other. Arsenal even played a snatch and grab game, defending for most of their away games, a quick raid from Bastin or Hulme, a single goal and off back to London with the points, leaving the local side's supporters with the illogical conviction that the best side had lost.

Thus Walsall's victory was heralded throughout the country, not just in the Black Country, and this was far more a reflection of the economic climate that any deep seated affection for that unattractive Staffordshire town. The game was, and remains, the perfect example of weak, underprivileged David rising to humiliate rich, overbearing Goliath.

THE MAGNIFICENT SEVEN

*Or how Ted Drake got his own back on the Aston Villa
crowd*

Tom Whittaker, Arsenal's trainer, had problems. The club
manager, George Allison, lay in hospital recovering from a
heart attack. Whittaker did not want to disturb him. But only
a couple of days before the away match against Arsenal's
traditional rivals, Aston Villa, his centre-forward Ted Drake
was struggling with a knee injury. If Whittaker could not mend
the young forward, he would have to interrupt Allison's
convalescence to name a replacement.

Whittaker was a physiotherapist with a remarkable reputation for healing, and Ted Drake trusted him implicitly. The
pair virtually lived in the treatment room as the trainer
manipulated his skilled hands to reduce the injury. Drake,
who was to spend many an hour receiving treatment during
his playing career, waited patiently. He would leave the
decision to Whittaker. Eventually the trainer came to his
decision. He wrapped strapping around the weak joint but
pronounced: 'You won't break down'. The kick-off was only
hours away.

That was just how close Ted Drake came to not appearing
at Villa Park on the afternoon of December 14 1935 – a day on
which he established a remarkable scoring record that has
lasted for more than 40 years. Arsenal beat their old rivals
by seven goals to one, and Ted Drake, carrying that support
around his left knee, scored all seven goals, from only eight
attempts at putting the ball into the net.

The result itself, despite its immense dimensions, scarcely
raised many eyebrows. After all, Aston Villa, for all their

pride, were bottom of the First Division. They had already revealed a defensive weakness which had cost them 52 goals in their previous 18 games; the Saturday before they entertained Arsenal they had been roundly thrashed by Manchester City by five clear goals. And if Arsenal trailed Sunderland by eight points at the more fancied end of the table, they still carried the reputation of a side which had won four Championships in the preceding five years. Though Alex James was missing from the team at Villa Park, names like Male, Hapgood, Copping, Bastin – and of course Drake – still stood out in the match programme.

The prospect of a look at Arsenal was no doubt partly responsible for Villa's largest crowd of the season – nearly 70,000. And the hope for the Villa fans lay in the arrival of expensively purchased newcomers, recruited to try to halt what had become a headlong plummet into Division Two. In the previous four weeks the Birmingham club had bought five players, the most expensive being George Cummings, a Scottish international left-back who had come south from Partick Thistle for a fee of £8000. Tommy Griffiths, a Welsh international, had been acquired from Middlesbrough, to play as a 'stopper' centre-half, for £5000. Jackie Williams, a winger from Huddersfield, had cost £2000, while £500 more than that went on Jack Palethorpe, who had been leading the Sheffield Wednesday attack. But the very latest arrival was Alex Massie, an established Scottish international wing-half who had won his reputation with Hearts. Another large cheque for the times – £5000 – had been written out by the Villa to secure his services.

The Arsenal match was to be the home debut for Massie, and also the first occasion on which all five of the new signings were to play together. But of the new boys, by far the most was expected of Tommy Griffith – the man who would mark Drake. Villa had been trying for almost two years to adapt to the system of the defensive centre-half, instituted at Highbury by Herbert Chapman. To aid their cause they had paid a lot of money to Portsmouth for Jimmy Allen, a tall defender who had represented England. But Allen's presence had provided no dam against the tide of scores which had been sweeping into the Villa goal. Now he had been given the blame and Griffiths came into the side as his replacement.

None of these statistics were likely to worry the retiring Drake as he prepared himself in the dressing-room. Chapman had signed the centre-forward in 1933 from Southampton, where he had combined football with his work as a gas meter inspector. He had settled in well at Highbury and in the 1934–35 season had led the First Division scorers with 42 goals. He had also won his first England cap late in 1934, when he was one of seven Arsenal men who took part in the notorious match against Italy which came to be known as the 'Battle of Highbury'. Drake scored in England's 3–2 success.

He had been fashioned straight from the mould of courageous centre-forwards. He was strong, and beautifully built at two inches under six feet tall and a pound or two under 13 stone. He was quick – a truly powerful runner – but above all he was brave. He would willingly plunge headlong into a packed goal area to try to divert the ball across the line; he would go crashing to the ground after desperate challenges from defenders, yet pick himself up and battle on; and he established something of a reputation for returning bandaged to the fray after being carried off following collisions of frightening dimension. His career was to be one long battle against injuries – struggles that he invariably won – and it was nothing less than appropriate that he should have shrugged off another knock when he ran on to the field that afternoon at Villa Park.

Of course it is the goals that stick in the memory, but Drake himself recalls another incident that he found relevant. 'In those days I believe that the pitches were slightly heavier than they are today. I think it was because teams used to train on them more than they do now. So they were subject to more use and had less time to recover. And because of this, we used to wear a very long stud. Well, I was wearing these studs against Aston Villa, and during the kick-in while we were warming up someone rolled a ball on to the hard core area that runs round the pitch. I went over to get it.'

'Well, my damned studs got caught on this hard core, and I stumbled and fell over. Their supporters loved it, of course. They jeered and yelled at me. I was slightly bruised and cut, but most of all I was mad at those supporters. I was wild. Really, they lost the match for themselves at that moment. I was determined to do something to get my own back.'

But, as in all the best stories, there was little hint of the drama ahead in the opening minutes of the match. Villa, despite the degree of unfamiliarity amongst their players, settled the quicker of the two sides. Left-half Wood contrived the initial strike at goal, a shot which passed close to the post. Massie's touch play was soon in evidence as he controlled an awkward ball instinctively and set Jackie Williams away along the right touchline. The winger's centre was cleared only as far as Massie, but another creative touch from the Scotsman was wasted by Ronnie Dix, the inside-left. Better scoring attempts were fashioned by Dai Astley, Massie himself, and then Dix as Arsenal's much-heralded defence sought to cope with the pressure from the home side.

Indeed, after ten minutes Villa should have taken the lead when Cummings swept the ball upfield to Palethorpe. Though the centre-forward was in position to run through at goal, he deflected the responsibility elsewhere with an unnecessary pass to a colleague. The gap that had half-opened was instantly closed. It was a hesitancy in attack which Drake was not to share.

On the quarter-hour, Drake claimed his first goal. His pace was ideally suited to the counter-thrust, and Arsenal finally broke free from the Villa pressure with a long ball from Pat Beasley. Drake out-paced Tommy Griffiths and showed none of Villa's caution in sight of the target. He finished his run with a powerful, accurate drive that gave Morton in the Villa goal no chance.

Villa rode the shock reasonably well, and continued to be the more aggressive side in every department except finishing. They pushed forward for another 13 minutes until they faced, and capitulated to, another Drake breakaway. This time he broke out on to a long pass from Cliff Bastin and again the goal owed much to Ted's speed. But it was also a testimony to his strength, for he withstood a determined challenge from Cummings and retained his balance before firing past the hapless Morton.

Drake remembers the similarity in the two opening goals: 'Both were fast breakaways and my greatest asset was definitely my pace. In both cases I'd got away and left the centre-half behind me. On the first goal I could see the two full-backs converging on the cover, but I beat them to the ball and scored. The second goal was very similar except that one of the full-backs got to me. But I brushed him aside and smacked it in.'

Almost half an hour played. Two Arsenal attacks. Two Drake shots. Two goals to nil. Inevitably up went the cry of 'lucky Arsenal', the chant that followed then throughout the 1930s and beyond. But Drake answered the taunt within six minutes to complete his first hat-trick with his third shot of the game. Some observers felt that he was waiting in an offside position when a shot from Beasley was deflected into his stride by a defender, but he did not hesitate and once again Morton was retrieving the ball from the back of his net.

Villa continued to attack – now out of blind necessity. They had been subjected to so many recent defeats that what confidence the players had begun the game with had been brittle; now Drake had completely shattered it. The forays that had started the match with a boiling intensity now wore a tepid air. Against the likes of Male and Hapgood, Herbie Roberts and the biting tackling of Wilf Copping, they were limited to a couple of half-chances, and even when they did put the ball into the Arsenal goal the score was disallowed for a foul by Palethorpe on Wilson. Arsenal, territorially defeated, went in three goals to the good at half-time.

Those Villa fans who spent the ten-minute break bemoaning their team's ill-fortune had little idea of the further blows that awaited them and their team. Drake, with already one hat-trick to his name, claimed another three goals in the opening 13 minutes of the second half. The first, his fourth, came in the 48th minute and owed much to a miscalculation from

Griffiths, who relaxed, thinking the ball was going to roll out of play. There was no such relaxation from the Arsenal centre-forward, who claimed it and immediately tucked it with great skill past Morton. Four shots, four goals, and Villa collapsed.

Two minutes later, inside-forwards Ray Bowden and Bastin interpassed through the demoralised Villa ranks before Bastin left the job of finishing the move to the man in form; Drake duly slammed in goal number five. Any ache in the knee was easily forgotten in the fulfilment of putting the Villa supporters in their places for that pre-match bout of derision. And when in the 58th minute a punch-drunk defender duly rolled a clearance to him on the edge of the penalty area, he happily cracked in number six.

Shortly afterwards, came the only blemish on Drake's day of robot-like finishing. Presented with another chance, he produced a shot which bulletted down off the underside of the bar and was cleared. But Drake was convinced that the referee and not the bar had denied him another goal: 'I hit the ball hard, and as it came down off the bar it hit the back of the goalkeeper's neck and somehow was scrambled clear. But I felt sure it was over the line, and I turned and claimed it for a goal. I told the referee that it was over the line, but he wouldn't have any of it.'

As if encouraged by Drake's one failure, Villa finally contrived a goal for themselves. Houghton crossed accurately into the goalmouth and Palethorpe placed his header past Wilson. Straight from the re-start Palethorpe almost broke through again, but it was Arsenal's only really anxious period in defence, a theme picked up in the following day's edition of the *Sunday Pictorial*: 'Wilson did not have an idle time in goal but most of the shots he had to deal with were of the hopeless variety. He was covered so well by the rest of the defence, and the Villa were such poor finishers, that one goal for the home side was about their due.'

Drake had still not finished, though he had to wait until the final minute for his seventh goal. Again Bastin was the provider and again the finishing was so precise. Now Drake had equalled the individual Division One scoring record set up by James Ross of Preston against Stoke in 1888, and he had established a new mark for a First Division forward in any away match.

As Drake turned on his way back for the final kick-off of the game he was not engulfed by his team-mates in the manner of more contemporary celebrations: 'In those days, shaking hands was the normal form of congratulations after a goal, but we tried to cut that out as well. Just a quick "Well done!" and we got on with the game. Anyway in those days I used to take everything in my stride. I didn't think I'd done anything really special. It was only afterwards, when everyone made such a fuss, that I realised that it was quite something.'

'After the game all 22 players signed the ball for me, which I felt was a tremendous thing for the Villa players to do after such a defeat. They were very kind, and I have never forgotten the way their club treated me on what was such a bad day for them. Whenever I have been there to watch a match, I have always been so respectful to them.'

But only one Villa player discussed the game at length with Ted Drake. And that was a man who had not taken part: 'Jimmy Allen came into the dressing-room and he thanked me for what I had done. He wasn't being naughty or anything, or being unfair to his team-mates. But he had been blamed for Villa doing so badly, and he'd been the man who had been dropped. And he just said that I had proved a point for him – that there were a lot of things wrong, and that it hadn't all been his fault. We had a chat about it. As for Tommy Griffiths, he didn't say anything to me at all.'

Drake had certainly fired the cannons which had sunk Aston Villa, and the newspapers of the day were full of allusions to that other Drake – Sir Francis. And Villa, like the Spaniards, had learned to their cost that success on the football field, as in war, cannot always be purchased. But for Ted Drake, the story did not quite end there.

That left knee, so nearly a barrier to the making of history, had suffered further damage during the game. And a few days later, Drake did break down and this time Tom Whittaker recommended hospitalisation and the removal of a cartilage. Indeed, one of Ted Drake's trademarks in the later years of his career became that eleastic bandage – worn for the first time at Villa Park – around the troublesome joint. He was out of football for ten weeks, one of the main reasons why Arsenal lost their League title to Sunderland and only finished in sixth place in the League. But they remained sufficiently successful to win through to the Cup Final. And Ted Drake was determined to be fit to play at Wembley.

'Of course, I had to prove myself in matches to stand a chance of selection for the Final against Sheffield United, and I remember playing in a friendly against Cambridge University, and then in a reserve match against Fulham and coming through without any problems. So I was picked to play again for the first team. And you can guess who it was against, can't you? It was the return match against Aston Villa. More than that they were in trouble, still at the bottom of the League, and if they didn't win at Highbury they would be relegated. Well, to cap it all, I headed a goal and put them down into the Second Division. I can remember running back after scoring and saying to their fellows that I was terribly sorry for what I had done!'

More than that, Ted Drake had proved his own fitness to play for Arsenal in the 1936 FA Cup Final. After such an absence through injury he might have been expected to settle just for a Wembley appearance. But the fairy-tale had one more chapter to run. As Arsenal fought out a taut struggle with Sheffield United, the final difference between the sides was just one goal – a header from Ted Drake.

Drake continued to batter away at goal with no concern for personal safety until another injury – this time to his spine – finally put paid to his playing career. Later he was to prove that his football skills had been intuitive as much as instinctive as a shrewd manager of Chelsea when they won the First Division Championship almost 20 years after his personal triumph at Villa Park. Later still, after an absence from the game, he joined Fulham as a much-respected chief scout.

But despite all his other achievements, he will always be

rightly remembered as the man who scored seven goals away from home in a First Division match. As the man who scored his seven goals from just eight attempts. And as the man who only just defied injury to do it.

THE MATTHEWS FINAL

Or how Bolton Wanderers scored three in a Wembley final
– and lost!

Since the FA Cup Final first went to Wembley in 1923, the match has nearly always produced moments worth remembering – a great goal, a disputed penalty, a giant-killing. But one stands out head and shoulders above the rest in national legend – the Matthews' Final. Rightly or wrongly, this has gone down as the greatest of them all – when the old maestro brought his team back from the dead and finally won his much cherished medal. The truth, however, is a little more complicated.

Blackpool did, in fact, come back from 3–1 down, scored twice in the last three minutes to provide the highest scoring Wembley Final, and left Bolton as the only losers ever to have scored three goals in a final. In fact in over 100 years only ten sides have scored more than three.

When Blackpool and Bolton went to Wembley, the Seasiders were favourites, in every sense, over their Lancastrian rivals. They had lost the finals of 1948 and 1951. Stanley Matthews, every schoolboy's hero, who had joined them from Stoke after World War II, was now 38, and this seemed to be his last chance of a major honour. In fact he was still playing League football ten years later, but that is part of another story.

His brilliant wing play, based on making the full-back believe that he would go inside, then chasing along the touchline and centring from the right for centre-forwards of the calibre of Lawton and Mortensen, was always a little inconsistent, and no doubt owed its extreme success to the rigid tactics of the time. The winger in those days was closely marked by the full-back; if he got free, then he was usually able to reach the goal-line and centre. There was none of the spacial retreat so common today. Nevertheless, Matthews perfected the winger's art and was probably the greatest of that sadly defunct breed; no doubt he would have been a great player in any age.

His unusual quality as a footballer was discovered early. He was a centre-half when he played for his school at 11 – certainly not a defensive one, because he scored eight goals one afternoon – but they soon made him into an outside-right, and within a year of the change, he was an office boy at Stoke City Football Club; at 15 he played two games with the reserves, and on his 17th birthday he signed as a professional, making his first-team debut in March 1932.

Through these years he was still under the severe eye of his father, who took charge of his money. With no bus fares, the boy walked the two miles between Hanley and Stoke every day, because the exercise was good for him; when he became a player, half his wages went into a Post Office savings account.

At 18 he was in the first team, Stoke City were promoted, and young Matthews won a Second Division Championship medal; at 19 he played for England. That first international, against Wales at Cardiff, was in September 1934; his last was to be against Scotland in April 1957, when he was over 40.

If Matthews had retained his place throughout that period he would have gained 119 caps in official matches. As it was he won 54 (plus 26 in wartime and victory games) in a rather sporadic international career. Indeed the start was not a good one: the first two displays, against Wales and Italy, even induced one of the leading football writers of the time to accuse him of 'slowness and hesitation' and to conclude that 'perhaps he has not got the big match temperament'.

But Matthews became a great star, and there was an intensely dramatic quality in the way his great performancss were matched to great occasions. Yet none of this was reflected in his personality off the field. There was no flamboyance, no distinction in his manner or his dress, little variety in the flat intonations of his voice, with its Potteries accent. His manner was understated and self-contained, his only interest the playing of football, his obsession that of physical fitness.

But he did have a precise notion of his value. He stayed 16 years with Stoke, and twice asked for a transfer. The first time produced an extraordinary local demonstration. Thousands of handbills and posters appeared all over the city, bearing the words 'Stanley Matthews Must Not Go', 3000 people attended a public protest meeting, and a thousand more paraded outside with placards. Matthews stayed for nine more years, and then, after being out for a few weeks through injury, he was asked to play in the reserves, rather than force a change in a winning team. He refused, and in 1947 he was transferred to Blackppol. He owned an hotel there (he was thrifty, as one might expect from his background), he trained on the Blackpool ground, during and after the war, and had made it clear he would go nowhere else. So Blackpool got him for what was even then a bargain price – £11,500.

Blackpool were seventh in the First Division in 1953, Bolton 14th. Both had relatively poor defences but more than adequate attacks, both including an England centre-forward. An attractive game was certainly in prospect.

Blackpool were rightly favoured, but Bolton still dominated the first two-thirds of the match. Within 75 seconds Blackpool's defensive frailty showed as a mediocre shot from Bolton's centre-forward Nat Lofthouse crept through Blackpool keeper George Farm's hands. Soon afterwards Lofthouse hit the post, but far worse for Bolton was left-half Eric Bell's injury. Substitutes were not allowed in those days, and he moved to the left-wing. Bolton reshuffled their side, but Blackpool took control in midfield and Stan Mortensen equalized after 35 minutes. The ball went in off Bolton's Hassall and he is sometimes credited (or debited) with an own goal. As it was going in anyway, the goal should rightly be given to Mortensen.

But four minutes later Bolton took back their lead when Moir headed in after Farm had failed to clear a high ball, and, soon into the second half, Bolton appeared to have made it safe when the injured Bell leapt to head a Holden centre home.

Blackpool's forwards had not had a good match so far. It was said afterwards that Matthews had to have a painkilling injection before the game, and he certainly did not come into his own until the last half-hour. No doubt assisted by the fact that left-back Ralph Banks was suffering with cramp, Matthews began to completely dominate that side of the field.

The ball kept coming out through Bolton's weakened quarter, and the crowd saw and loved 30 minutes of Matthews' feints and darts. Bolton took no extra precautions and, with 22 minutes left, paid the price. A Matthews' centre was dropped by keeper Hanson for Mortensen to force home. Twenty-two minutes seemed enough to the crowd willing Blackpool on at Wembley, and the millions watching on television, but Bolton were coping, and Matthews' passes were wasted. According to referee Mervyn Griffiths, there were only two seconds of normal time left when Mortensen scored the equalizer with a free-kick from the edge of the penalty area. There seemed no way through, but Mortensen had his third – the only Cup final hat-trick this century.

For the two minutes of injury time, the ball seemed to be continuously at Matthews' feet. Down the wing he went, finally rounding Banks and then centre-half Barrass, only to stumble as he reached the goal-line. But, somehow, the ball came back. It was not a good centre, running along the ground, but it got through to Bill Perry, who it hit home with less than 60 seconds left to play. The game had become a fairy tale, Matthews had his medal.

The legend has grown since. Television flashbacks invariably show the last few minutes, ignoring the previous 85. It is certainly arguable that Bolton threw away the match, rather than Blackpool succeeded in winning it. When Bell was injured they moved Harry Hassall, the inside-left, back to left-half. He was not a particularly good tackler and did not control the side of the field that was Blackpool's most dangerous. It possibly also left Bolton short of punch moving forward against a poor defence (though they did score twice afterwards). Thus when the ten fit Trotters tired towards the end, Matthews found himself facing an inside-left playing as tackling midfield man and a full-back half-crippled with cramp.

Ernie Taylor, Blackpool's midfield schemer, was later very critical of the tactical switch that led to Harry Hassall moving to left-half. 'They gave it to us,' he said. 'They should have switched their team around differently when Bell was hurt. They should have moved Johnny Wheeler across from right-half. Wheeler was a good defender. Taking Hassall out of the attack left them short of punch. I don't know what their manager was playing at.'

Hassall's place in the forward line was taken by Langton, a player who had made his debut 16 years earlier. Langton found it too strenuous a role on a hot afternoon at Wembley on the most tiring of pitches.

Taylor was not the only person to criticize Bolton's tactics when Bell was injured. His manager, Joe Smith – a Bolton player for 16 years – maintained that right-winger Doug Holden should have gone to the left, to do the harrying that Langton could not manage, and that the full-backs should have been exchanged as well.

And Bolton's attempts to protect their 3–1 lead would be viewed with scorn were they to be used in a modern Cup final. Long kicks upfield were promptly returned. (Lofthouse was badly shaken in a fall, and was extremely well handled by skipper Harry Johnston.) And although Lofthouse and other Bolton players repeatedly kicked into touch, there was none of the possession play now so evident. Nor – to Bolton's credit – was there any 'professional fouling' of Matthews. Indeed, Bolton's players acted throughout with commendable sportsmanship, never more so than in the last desperate stages.

Bolton manager Bill Ridding admitted in a radio interview that he had not given special instructions to his players on how to deal with Matthews. According to Lofthouse, the gist of Ridding's pre-match talk was, 'I'm not going to tell you how to play, but try to dictate the game.' Ridding was perhaps in step with the rest of his managerial colleagues of the time. The game was different then. The examination of opponents, the study and exploitation of weaknesses, these were not considered on the scale they are today. The players were simply left to play as they saw fit.

In fact, of the six popular daily papers, only one made any reference in the after-match reports to Bolton's tactics. Accounts of the game consisted mainly of sympathy for the losers and indulgent praise for the winners – Matthews in particular, 'scribbling with his fantastic feet the greatest Cup Final story of all time', as one newspaper wrote.

Looking back, the facts suggest that this was exaggeration indeed. Banks, the defender marking Matthews, was little more than a cripple who would have been unable to stop any winger. 'Once Banks was limping,' Matthews told reporters after the match, 'I knew our chance was to keep hammering away at the weak spot.' Yet Matthews failed to take complete advantage of this opportunity, most of his crosses dropping harmlessly over the bar, and his pass to Perry in injury time was really a miskick delivered as he lost his balance and fell.

Matthews himself later said, 'It was my greatest day, but I didn't win the match on my own.' Ernie Taylor certainly agrees with that. 'Our hero was Morty,' he says. 'The notion that it was a one-man match is sentimental nonsense. The idea has grown over the years. I know how well Stan played – for part of the match. But he needed others to back him up.'

In recent years, in reappraising the final, it has been suggested that Matthews' performance on the day did not win the game, rather it was the legend built up over two decades that paralysed Bolton and gave Blackpool their inspiration.

While not denying the great value of a legendary player, even past his best, that analysis is surely suspect. Bolton were patently *not* terrorized by Matthews – they made no attempt to swap full-backs or put extra players on him even when both their left-sided defenders were clearly unable to perform their jobs. And if they were paralysed, then it was by their own misfortune in losing the full fitness of two key players and, of course, by Stanley Mortensen's hat-trick.

And that is the remarkable thing about this match. Dramatically exciting it certainly was, a great footballing exhibition certainly not. But it was Mortensen who won it with the only Cup Final hat-trick this century – and a 'pure' one–two–three at that. And yet his contribution is almost forgotten, submerged in the Matthews' legend. Things are not always as they seem, even in football.

PRIDE BEFORE A FALL

How the magnificent Magyars destroyed England's delusions of grandeur

The cliché 'the end of an era' could have been created for the events of November 23 1953 at Wembley Stadium. For England, the greyness of that afternoon was reflected in 90 minutes of desolation which ended one of the nation's proudest records. Not in the entire history of international football, a span of 81 years, had a team of foreigners come to these shores and departed victorious. Not, that is, until the arrival of Hungary, the magnificent Magyars.

It was certainly typical of the times that the side from Eastern Europe were regarded as simply another in a succession of opponents who really could not expect anything other than defeat at Wembley. Although England had hardly set the world on fire with their first ever World Cup venture three years earlier, and had indeed been disgraced at Belo Horizonte by the stunning 1–0 defeat by the United States, the prevailing thought of the day was that in England we were the best at a game of which we were the tutors, whilst most other nations remained the pupils.

It was a narrow-minded attitude, a case of pride heading for a fall. It ignored several nerve-tingling escapes. Almost three years earlier to the day, Yugoslavia had earned a 2–2 draw at Highbury, a result repeated by a no-more-than-average French side 11 months later, also on the Arsenal ground. Sandwiched in between had been many an anxious moment at Wembley when Argentina were the visitors – the South American side had led until the last 11 minutes, when Mortensen scored twice to preserve dignity and the unbeaten record.

In November 1951, Austria, inspired by the brilliant

Hanappi and Ocwirk, also shared the spoils at Wembley, though this time it was the visitors who needed a late goal after they had taken the lead. And two years later, just a month before Hungary's visit, defeat stared England in the face until a contentious penalty was converted by Alf Ramsey, in the dying moments of an international against the Rest of Europe, to earn a 4-4 draw.

After that scare England had one more fixture before Hungary came to Wembley, a Home International game against Northern Ireland at Goodison Park, which they won comfortably enough by three goals to one. But the selectors saw fit to make changes from that victorious side. Only one alteration was made in defence, with as expected, Ramsey returning to the exclusion of Rickaby of West Bromwich Albion, who had been his deputy at Goodison. But only Matthews retained his place in attack. Quixall and Hassall, the two inside forwards, gave way to Ernie Taylor, the diminutive Blackpool man who was Matthews' club partner and who was gaining his first cap, and Jackie Sewell, who had been out of the side for a year. At centre-forward Lofthouse was replaced by a third Blackpool player, Stan Mortensen, while at outside-left George Robb, the amateur international from Tottenham Hotspur, took over from Jimmy Mullen. Robb had been the subject of a press campaign in London and may well have earned his selection as a result of the support of Fleet Street.

So if England were not exactly a scratch side, they were hardly a team in the sense of the Hungarians, whose players had been together for several years in a way unheard of before in world football and in a manner totally abhorrent to the thinking of the Football Association. Before any other nation, Hungary had realised that team play at international level depended on the sort of blend that only comes from regular practice and training sessions together. Whereas England's players met at most a couple of days before a match and then not again until a matter of hours before the game, Hungary's squad had been together for years, spending weeks away from their clubs at training centres; they had been the first country to run their national team as a club side.

The virtue of their ways had been proven well before their fixture at Wembley. Their last defeat had been on May 14 1950 – a 5–3 beating by Austria – and in their unbeaten run which was to span 29 games until their remarkable defeat by Germany in the 1954 World Cup final, they had won the Olympic Games gold medal in Helsinki. Most of that side came to play against England, among them brilliant artists like Ferenc Puskas, a goalscoring inside-forward with a marvellous left foot, Sandor Kocsis, masterful in the air and nicknamed 'the Golden Head', Nandor Hidegkuti, a creative centre-forward, and Josef Bozsik, another intuitive wing-half.

But in 1953 England's attitudes remained insular. Few continental players were known by name; instead their attributes were covered by bland generalisations like 'they can't shoot' or 'they don't like physical challenge' and certainly they were not regarded as any real match for the pride of the home country. Moreover, England's tactical approach on the field had remained unaltered for 20 years; come what may, there would be a goalkeeper, two full-backs, three half-backs, and five forwards – the WM echelon was the only way an Englishman knew how to play. The Hungarians would prove the folly of the rigidity of such thinking.

But even the confident Hungarians had to cope with the pressures of a Wembley occasion, with 100,000 partisan supporters against them. Ferenc Puskas, in his autobiography *Captain of Hungary*, recalls, 'Looking round our dressing-room I saw nothing but preoccupied players trying to disguise their nervousness. But I felt a bit happier when I glanced into the English players' dressing-room and saw the same tension. So on the count of nerves we were to start with equal chances.' Within 60 seconds of the kick-off those odds were to change dramatically – in Hungary's favour.

Scarcely had an England player touched the ball when Bozsik and Zakarias instigated a central attack. The third player in the move was Hidegkuti, wearing a white number nine on the back of his cherry red shirt. From 25 yards he made space with a quick dummy and powered a lifting drive beyond Merrick's right hand and into the top corner of the England net –

an instant answer to those whose belief in England's invincibility was based on the premise that continentals could not shoot.

So much did Hungary have of the ball in those opening minutes that the defenders looked shell-shocked at such an opening volley. But the truth was that they were beginning to realise their own inability to cope with a tactical formation that was beyond their comprehension. Hidegkuti was the key. He wore number nine, which to every self-respecting footballer of the day meant that he played centre-forward; at the very vanguard of every attack, he would be expected to be an out-and-out attacker, and he would be the responsibility of the centre-half.

But Hidegkuti exhibited a different version of the role. He played deeper, dropping back into areas which normally belonged exclusively to wing-halves and inside-forwards. Harry Johnston, England's centre-half, could never come to terms with this perplexing problem. If he followed Hidegkuti he would find himself pulled out of the heart of his defence; if he remained there, Hidegkuti was allowed to run free.

Billy Wright, England's captain on the day and at wing-half very close to the problem, remembers the confusion: 'We had never come up against this sort of tactic before. But suddenly we were chasing shadows. Harry Johnston stayed back as cover and no one picked up Hidegkuti. He caused all the confusion.' Within minutes of his first goal, Hidegkuti had the ball in the net again after Czibor, on the left wing, and Puskas had scissored an opening, but the Dutch referee Leo Horn caught a Hungarian forward offside.

Then, remarkably, England were level. Ironically it was Johnston who manufactured the chance. In his own penalty area he intercepted one of the few loose Hungarian attacks and carried the ball forward before releasing a beautifully weighted pass to his Blackpool team-mate Mortensen; the centre-forward in his turn freed Sewell on his left and the Sheffield Wednesday inside forward, at £35,000 the most expensive British player of the day, shot left-footed and low past Grosics.

If the move offered a ray of hope that the Hungarians could

not match the brilliant skills of their attack with substance in defence, that ray was but a faint glimmer within half-an-hour. In this period Hungary scored three times as Wright and Dickinson, the two wing-halves, fought in vain to cope with the succession of attacks initiated by the unattended Hidegkuti. Moreover, it was Hidegkuti himself who restored the Magyar lead. Czibor's pace down the touchline was unsettling both full-backs and from a precise cross Kocsis deflected the ball with his dangerous head, to Hidegkuti, whose shot found the net despite Eckersley's concerted efforts to block it.

Now Czibor switched to the right wing and Kocsis sent him sprinting past Eckersley. As the low cross came over Puskas sprinted towards the near post. Wright, his faithful marker, traced the same path and by positioning himself between Puskas and the goal appeared to have done his job. What followed was pure magic.

Puskas excessively favoured his left foot but there seemed no way he could get a shot on target without having to resort to his right. Wright moved in to block that eventuality and found himself tackling thin air. Puskas in full flight had killed the ball, checked to an absolute standstill and rolled the ball backwards with the sole of his left boot. Wright, utterly defeated by the cheek of the ploy, surged past and at that moment was out of the game. Instantly Puskas readjusted his balance with the goal before him and the ball at the end of his left boot. With the ruthlessness of a hired gun he thrashed his shot past Merrick. It was all over in a fraction of a second; Merrick had no time to move off his line to smother the ball and cut down the angle; Wright had barely time to look round and witness the finish.

If that was pure skill there was a certain amount of luck attached to the next sledgehammer blow to England's hopes. Yet another red-shirted attack was repelled 25 yards from England's goal at the cost of a free-kick. Bozsik's blast at Merrick's goal might well have missed its target until the ball struck Puskas on the heel and flew in past the stranded goalkeeper. England's invincible army now trailed 4–1 on her own battlefield.

If England were finding themselves inferior in individual

ability and collective organisation, they did not let courage desert them. Grosics had to find a great plunging save to rebuff a header from George Robb, and then the Hungarian goalkeeper was beaten for a second time. In many ways it was a goal which typified the difference in class between the two sides. Hungary's attack had been a rapier, but now England bludgeoned a score with Mortensen battling past a couple of defenders, accelerating clear, and shooting decisively.

Billy Wright remembers the mood in the half-time dressing-room; 'We were all a bit shattered but there was nothing dramatic we could do to change things. I just kept saying that Hidegkuti was the problem, and that he had to be marked. We urged our inside-forwards to try and keep track of him. All their players had had so much space.'

If the players felt that there was any chance of a revival, their hopes lay in ruins within ten minutes of the resumption. Merrick was instantly in action diving to turn Czibor's header on to a post. From the scramble the ball was layed back to Bozsik who this time needed no deflection to find the net, Merrick being hopelessly beaten by a beautifully struck rising drive. 5-2 to Hungary with barely half the match over. Now defeat was inevitable and a complete rout a probability.

The sixth goal followed in the next attack. Fittingly it fell to Hidegkuti, whose personal performance, even allowing for England's inadequate attempts to contain him, had been of the highest calibre. Puskas' controlled lob was met with a volley of equal stature and once again Merrick might as well have been on the terraces behind his goal for all the chance he had to prevent the score. As the Hungarians hugged the scorer on his hat-trick, Grosics performed cartwheels in the opposite goalmouth.

England managed a third reply after a sortie in which the gallant Mortensen again played the leading part. Finally he was sent sprawling inside Hungary's penalty area and Mr Horn's decision enabled Alf Ramsey to put his name on the score sheet in what turned out to be his final international appearance.

With still half-an-hour to play the odds were on England having to endure further humiliations as the brilliant Hungarians mixed short and long passes to knife their way in on

Merrick's goal. But chances frittered away as if the fates had decreed that enough was enough, even though there was little indication that the England ranks had in any way come to terms with the difficulties.

The inflexibility of the English game had been thoroughly exposed by a side which had chosen to play four defenders in a line across their goal, two creative players as midfield linkmen, Boszik and Hidegkuti, with four attacking forwards in Kocsis, Puskas, and the two wingers, Budai and Czibor. In contrast, Hungary's flexibility had been all too apparent with Hidegkuti freeing himself from his deep-lying role to claim three goals and Boszik similarly scoring once and being significantly involved in one of Puskas' two goals.

Billy Wright was only too aware of the shortcomings of England's approach to the game: 'We were shown to be out of date in so many ways. To start with, they were in essence a very good club side. They had all played together for such a long time and their fluency was the result of knowing each other so well. I think they would have beaten us for that reason alone, even if we could have coped with their deep-lying centre-forward. But in fact we were a not-so-good club side. Our defence had played together I know, but that was all really. I don't honestly think that we had the best players available in our side, but that isn't an excuse.'

'They were so much better than us on the day. But I suppose if they did have a weakness it was in defence. After all, we did manage to score three goals against them and put their defence under some pressure. Unfortunately, we just couldn't get enough of the ball to do more damage.'

Puskas, in his autobiography, made some equally telling post-match comments: 'Late in the match Hidegkuti was shadowed by both Wright and Dickinson, but in doing this they left Kocsis and myself unguarded. Our positioning and what might be called the "retreating attacks" led by our centre-forward completely shattered the England defence.

'Throughout the game we demonstrated the golden rule of modern football and that is: the good player keeps playing even without the ball. All the time he is placing himself so that when the ball comes to him he is able to make good use of it. In some measure we improved the English saying "Kick and run" to "pass accurately and run into a good position".

'We didn't nurse the ball, but kept passing it so quickly that an onlooker might have thought that the ball was burning our feet. But however quickly we got rid of it we saw that it usually went to one of our side. This quick game, combined with the fact that we had freed ourselves from the burden of the old-fashioned rule of staying in one's original position, did much to tire England's defence.'

Sadly, this shattering blow to the pride of England's football had little immediate effect. It spelt the end of several international careers: Ramsey's appearance, his 32nd in an England shirt, was his last; Bill Eckersley, his partner on several occasions, was also discarded, after the grilling he had suffered from Czibor and Budai; Harry Johnston, bemused and taunted by Hidegkuti, never played for his country again; Ernie Taylor, brought in to prompt his Blackpool partner Matthews, lost his place, his first cap also his last; Stan Mortensen, despite his whole-hearted endeavour, was by now a veteran and the 90 minutes against Hungary marked his final performance in an international; and George Robb had not justified the faith placed in him by the selectors or by the Fleet Street writers who had backed him, and he, too, never played for England again.

Merrick, Wright, Dickinson, and Sewell survived to play in the return game in Budapest the following May, a warm-up fixture for both countries before the 1954 World Cup in Switzerland. But England had learned little from the first meeting. A similar Hungarian side wreaked similar havoc, and the Budapest crowd was treated to a 7-1 annihilation.

Billy Wright was again subjected to a harrowing experience: 'It would be nice to remember that they got their seven goals in seven breakaway attacks, but in fact they slaughtered us. We were still inflexible in our tactical approach and still short-sighted about our approach to international football. We had not heeded the lessons. Their preparation for matches and whole attitude was much more professional. The feeling still prevailed that whatever the results British was still best and that in the end things would naturally come right again. But of course they did not.'

England's eventual failure in the 1954 World Cup, when they could not qualify from a Group with Belgium, Uruguay, and Switzerland, also failed to stimulate any real change of attitude – a policy epitomised by selectors not involved in professional football picking the side rather than a full-time manager. Not until Ramsey returned as manager nearly a decade later was England's international attitude brought into line with the more advanced thinking of other nations.

So though England's defeat at Wembley by Hungary was statistically the end of an era, in philosophical terms it was only the beginning of the new dawn.

THROWN TO THE WOLVES

*How the men at Molyneux restored England's shattered
pride in a very significant 'friendly'*

'I may never live to see a greater thriller than this. And if I see
many more as thrilling, I may not live much longer anyway.'
So wrote the celebrated sports journalist, Peter Wilson, in
the *Daily Mirror* on the morning of Tuesday, December 14
1954.

He was referring to Wolverhampton Wanderers' dramatic
3–2 victory the previous evening over Honved, the champion
club side of Hungary – a match not only of pulsating excitement but also of great prestige. Within the previous 13 months
the Hungarian national side had twice annihilated England,
emphasising the paucity of home-grown football skills; Honved brought to England the reputation of being the best club
side in the world and at Molineux fielded six of the team that
had beaten England at Wembley, five of whom had been in the
side that had unluckily lost the World Cup final to Germany a
matter of months earlier. By beating them, Wolves had fed an
audience desperately starved of success.

That Honved had come to England at all was a sign of chan-
ging times. Midweek friendlies under floodlights were a new
phenomenon. The appeal of matches against 'foreigners' also
had recent origins – until Hungary's magical talents had forced
a hurried reassessment of opinion, any side from outside Britain had been regarded as mere cannon-fodder. But by late
1954 visiting players from the continent had a new image, that
of mysterious conjurors who could in a football sense produce
rabbits from a hat with their almost surrealistic range of skills –
an image heightened by their appearance under the newfangled
glare of floodlighting. To the paying customers of the day they

were not so much visitors from another country as creatures from another planet.

Wolverhampton Wanderers, under the strict guidance of their former centre-half Stan Cullis, embodied much of the contemporary British style. Their players were strong, they were fit, and they outran and outchased most of their domestic opposition; their direct, attacking style based heavily on the use of the long pass, thrilled packed houses at Molineux. But the club had an outlook which stretched beyond the British insularity of the times.

They had recognised the possibilities of inviting the best of Europe's club sides to participate in friendly fixtures. The Austrian club side First Vienna, Maccabi from Israel, and then the heralded Moscow Spartak accepted the invitations, and Wolves' 4-0 hammering of the much-vaunted Russians provided the ideal fore-runner to the visit of Honved.

The whole of Britain licked its lips in anticipation of the conflict which was to provide a third confrontation between Billy Wright, captain of England, and Ferenc Puskas, captain of Hungary. Sixty thousand fans were locked into Molineux on the night, and as further proof of the prestige of the occasion, television cameras provided live coverage for those who could not be present.

In addition to Puskas, Honved fielded Budai and Czibor, the two wingers who had ended the international careers of Ramsey and Eckersley at Wembley; Kocsis, now recognised as the world's most dangerous striker in the air; Boszik, the superbly creative ally of Hidegkuti in the destruction of England, and Lorant, the forceful defender.

Wolves, too, had their stars. Bert Williams, though approaching the end of his career, was England's current goalkeeper; right-half Bill Slater had also been in the England team that had beaten world champions West Germany two weeks earlier, while left-half Ron Flowers was to begin his long international service within the next six months. In the forward line Johnny Hancocks and Denis Wilshaw had also worn England shirts, while Peter Broadbent would do so in the future. And, of course, at the hub of it all, stood the inspirational figure of

Billy Wright, who by now had made the transition to centre-half for both club and country.

December had arrived with characteristic greyness, and on the night of the 13th the pitch was heavy and muddy. Honved took the field in an all-white strip with three horizontal hoops in the centre of the shirts – a totally un-English outfit which immediately heightened the mystique of the foreigners, a feeling which their pre-match gesture of tossing flowers to the crowd did little to dissipate.

The fluence exercised by these conjurors extended over the Wolves players themselves as the Hungarian ball-artists made light of the cloying conditions and immediately put pressure on Williams' goal. One staccato burst of crisp, short, interpassing was only ended by the goalkeeper's brave dive at the feet of a Honved forward.

Honved continued to work the spell, and after ten minutes the wizardry took effect. Machos, shadowed by Flowers on the left-hand side of Wolves' defence, played in a cross which struck the defender and referee Reg Leafe from Nottingham awarded a free-kick for handball. Puskas took it with his inevitable left foot and placed a seven-iron chip on to the head of Kocsis, who unveiled the reasoning behind his nickname of the 'golden head' by butting the ball emphatically past Williams.

Immediately Wolves had the chance to equalise. Roy Swinbourne, Wolves' leading scorer, capitalised on a moment of relaxation in Honved's defence and saw the white of the Hungarian goal. But he snatched at the chance, shot against goalkeeper Farago, and the opportunity had passed.

Instantly, it looked a costly miss. Kocsis, already a scorer, adopted a creative mantle and curved a pass of perception and accuracy into the path of Machos. The Honved forward lengthened his stride, leaving Wright almost pathetically chasing behind him, and as Williams advanced, he thrashed the ball past him. Fourteen minutes had passed. Honved led by two goals. And if the Wolverhampton crowd was understandably subdued, they were not shocked; many had come expecting such majesty.

Their lead established, the Hungarians relaxed, but they

found that the Wolves players were far from daunted by the prospect of total annihilation. If anything, they stepped up the pace and, swinging the ball from flank to flank, they began to stretch Honved's defence.

But again chances brought no reward. Les Smith, the left winger, might have reduced the deficit when Farago could only push out an effort by Wilshaw, but as the opening manifested itself, Smith hesitated and was robbed, the moment evaporating. Farago by now was the more employed goalkeeper and as the home side sustained the pressure he proved that the magic was not confined to Honved's attack with dramatic saves from Flowers, Broadbent, Swinbourne, and then Smith – an agile stop denied the winger when he must have thought for an instant that he had redeemed his earlier miss.

But it was Williams who made the last save of the half; preventing a three-goal Honved lead which surely would have carried them safely through any amount of ravaging from the Wolves attack. Yet the save was made and at half-time the odds on a recovery were long but not hopeless.

The second half began in a cacophonous atmosphere and Wolves, superfit, steamrollered forward in a manner which had continuously overcome their English rivals. Inside four minutes they tasted fruit, though in a contentious manner. Johnny Hancocks carried the ball at left-back Kovacs and when the defender made an unfair challenge, both players were inside the penalty area. To most eyes the offence was mere obstruction, but referee Leafe adjudged pushing and instead of an indirect free-kick that the Honved players expected, they found themselves on the wrong end of a penalty kick.

Only five foot four inches tall and wearing size four boots, Hancocks was not cast in the usual mould of a penalty expert. But his ferocious shooting from the spot had rarely let his club down and now he drove low and powerfully, way past Farago's right hand. The crowd, already partisan, now bellowed in total commitment.

Having tasted blood, Wolves now scented a kill. Honved, so composed in the early stages, began to reel as somehow the home side found yet another gear as they surged forward. The

Amazing scenes at the first Wembley Cup final in 1923. PC Scorey and his white horse, Billy, can clearly be seen edging the crowd back towards the touchline so that the game can be started.

Hughie Gallacher, one of Scotland's 'Wembley Wizards'.
Known as the 'Wee Man', Gallacher was one of Scotland's
greatest forwards, but when his playing days were over he
sadly declined, and eventually committed suicide.

**Dixie Dean takes the field for Everton during the season
when he scored 60 goals in League football – a record unlikely
ever to be beaten.**

Arsenal's Ted Drake in scoring mood for the Gunners at Highbury in 1937. His left knee is bandaged – a reminder of the day he scored seven goals against Aston Villa at Villa Park.

Hungarians were no longer allowed to settle on the ball and keep possession. The pack was now in full cry.

Indeed the play became too frenetic. Corners looped in on Farago's goal, but over-enthusiasm continued to blunt the edge of Wolves' attack. But the near misses did nothing to heighten the visitors' confidence, and as their nervousness became increasingly apparent, it was clear that Wolves now had a real chance of not just equalising but going on to win.

They achieved both aims in the space of two minutes with under a quarter of an hour to play. In the 76th minute came a goal in vintage Wolves style. The inevitable long ball came from Slater who, unhindered by the heavy ball and uncertain foothold, swung a perfect pass out to Wilshaw on the left. The inside forward manipulated it past a defender and swung a probing cross into the goalmouth. There, amidst slithering chaos, Swinbourne plotted its course most accurately and when the ball dropped he reached it unmarked and headed past Farago who had started to come off his line.

The bedlam touched new decibel levels. No sooner had Honved kicked off than the home side mounted another attack, roared on by the baying masses. It was an irresistible combination. Wilshaw found space again and this time sped towards Honved's goal. As a defender moved out to challenge him he released a beautifully timed short pass inside to Swinbourne. The centre forward met it in full stride and slashed his shot inside Farago's left-hand post. With 12 minutes left, Wolves now led.

Honved were stung to retaliation as they fought their way against the succession of attacks like men walking into a gale force wind, and they created one painful moment as the crowd waited to fête their heroes. Czibor wriggled his way into a scoring position but Williams, after a quiet second period, alertly blocked the chance. Then Mr Leafe blew the final whistle, and spectators streamed on to the mud in a euphoria of congratulation.

It was an occasion that lent itself to superlatives. After the game Stan Cullis said, 'The match was the most exciting I have ever seen.' Wilshaw's reaction typified the feelings of the

Wolves players, 'It was the greatest game in which I have ever played.' But if the throbbing excitement of the 90 minutes deserved such fulsome praise, the conclusions drawn from the result had less validity.

Suddenly the headlines declared Wolves as champions of the world. Everywhere inside the country opinion prevailed that England's wobbling status in the universe of football had been saved. On one result all the shortcomings of the English games, so recently exposed at international level, seemed to be forgotten. Wolves indeed were adjudged to have overrun the entire Hungarian national team.

It was a shortsighted view. Honved were at the end of a tiring club tour, and Puskas and the rest of the internationals had finished a year of continual top-class play; indeed, only a week earlier several Honved players had been in the Hungarian team which had played an international against Scotland on a sapping pitch at Hampden Park. Without detracting from the Wolverhampton performance, their incentive to win had been so much greater than Honved's, though to the credit of Cullis' side, it had learned from England's experience.

Twenty years later, Billy Wright remembered the tactical improvements: 'I warned our inside-forwards to pick up their deep-lying centre-forward, and they did a great job. But I think the real difference in our performance compared to England's was that we played as a unit; we played as a club side, which England didn't. All over the pitch we marked properly, and in the end it stifled them. And of course we were a very fit side, and finally we wore them down.

'In those days, too, the Wolves side had great strength of character. When we were down we were really at our best. And of course the result brought tremendous prestige both to the players and to the club.'

If the patriotic chauvinism that greeted Wolves' triumph obscured and hindered the advance of British football, the ballyhoo which surrounded the result had a dramatic effect on the widening of the frontiers of competition. The boast that Wolves were the best team in Europe fell on disbelieving ears on the continent, among them one man of particular vision.

Gabriel Hanot, editor of the French sports magazine *L'Equipe*, had for a long time been a champion for the cause of a tournament between the top European clubs. Rightly he declared that Wolves would have to beat Honved in Budapest and also Spartak in Moscow before they could call themselves champions of Europe let alone champions of the world. The time was ripe for competition.

L'Equipe duly published a format for a European Cup, but the governing bodies of FIFA and UEFA offered only a luke-warm response. Undeterred, Hanot stepped up the campaign, and called a meeting of representatives from all the major European Leagues. Faced by the strong possibility of a breakaway tournament being established, football's bureau-cracy adopted a more radical attitude and finally both FIFA and UEFA added their official blessing. Almost all of *L'Equipe*s proposals were accepted, except that the competition was officially named the European Champion Clubs Cup rather than the European Cup, and the tournament was born at the start of the 1955–56 season.

Sadly, neither Wolverhampton Wanderers nor Honved were among the clubs invited to participate after giving a per-formance which had provided such a stimulus to the concept of European football. Wolves, League champions in 1954, had lost their title after meeting Honved, and Chelsea had shown more consistency to top the table. The Football League, how-ever, refused to allow Chelsea's entry, fearing that the extra fixtures would clutter up the League programme. But behind the decision lurked another sense of misgiving, that Chelsea, arguably the least distinguished side to win the League Championship in the 1950s, would not be a credit to the British game. Had Wolves, who finished runners-up in the League, been invited to compete, permission may well have been granted.

As for Honved, their place went to Red Banner, another skilled team from Budapest, who comprehensively beat Ander-lecht in their first tie but lost to the eventual runners-up Stade de Reims in the second round. But the following year Honved carried the flag of Hungary into the second tournament. That

67

year, 1956, was to have special significance in Hungarian history, and the Honved team found themselves in the centre of political tragedy.

In the October Puskas took his team to Spain to play the away leg of a tie against Atlético Bilbao. Before the match took place Hungary was overrun by Russian tanks, the government overthrown, and many of the team's families and friends were placed in grave danger. The players at first decided not to return, they played and lost 2–3 in Bilbao and then drew the second leg 3–3, a game which was played in Brussels, and which Honved would most certainly have won had not Farago broken his collar bone and Czibor gone in goal.

For months the team became footballing vagabonds, a touring circus earning their living from friendlies in Spain, Germany, Italy, and then Brazil. But in the end, Boszik, a government official, persuaded most of the players to return home. Only Puskas, Czibor, and Kocsis stayed in exile, tempted no doubt by the money they could earn in Spain or Italy. Puskas was almost penniless when Real Madrid finally took the gamble of signing him, and he became a key figure in the first great European club side, winners of the first five European Cups. Kocsis and Czibor eventually settled in Barcelona, where they were also essential ingredients in the emergence of another distinguished club side. But for Honved, it was an end to greatness.

Denied the chance of competing in Europe when their confidence was at its highest after their success in this series of friendlies, Wolves had to wait until they won the Championship in 1958 before they qualified for entry, and then they were summarily dismissed from the 1958–59 European Cup in their first match. They drew 2–2 at Molineux with Schalke 04 from West Germany but lost the second leg by the odd goal in three.

They retained their League title to earn themselves a second appearance the following year, and made reasonable early progress. They beat Vorwarts Berlin 3–2 on aggregate after losing in East Germany, and then convincingly eliminated Red Star Belgrade by three clear goals. But those who yet again proclaimed Wolves as world Champions were silenced by a display which evoked more than a passing memory of that grey day in December 1954.

Wolves had already lost 4–0 in Barcelona in the first leg of the second round of the competition, and recalled to the Spanish side for the second leg was Sandor Kocsis. As Barcelona totally mastered the English champions to record a devastating 5–2 win, Kocsis scored four times, and must have smirked in revenge each time that ball hit the back of the net.

In essence, there never was any real substance to the claim that the Wolves' win over Honved put British football back on the map. But at the end of a decade of disillusionment and much swallowing of pride for British football, their swaggering performance in the Molineux mud provided perhaps the happiest memory.

BUSINESS AS USUAL

The night that Manchester United picked up the pieces

The City of Munich has many memories for 20th century man. It was where Chamberlain and Daladier gave away Czechoslovakia in 1938, and the scene of the Olympic massacre of 1972. But for English football, the word has just one meaning. For it was at Munich's Reim Airport that, on February 6 1958, England lost the best club side she had probably ever had.

The cause was the failure of a British European Airways Elizabethan aircraft, named 'Lord Burghley', to take off in ice, snow, and, most important, slush after two previous attempts. To begin with it looked as though the living would outnumber the dead after the plane had ploughed through a house at the end of the runway and broken in half, but when the epitaphs came to be written, eight United players had died, including three current England internationals in captain Roger Byrne, centre-forward Tommy Taylor and the incomparable Duncan Edwards. Dead, too, were Walter Crickmer, the club secretary, coach Herbert Whalley, and trainer Tom Curry. Twelve others perished, including the ex-England goalkeeper Frank Swift, then a reporter for the *News of the World*.

Jackie Blanchflower, brother of Danny and Northern Ireland's centre-half, who had played in goal in the 1957 Cup Final when goalkeeper Ray Wood was carried off, and Johnny Berry, the winger who had represented England, never played football again. Only one sports writer, Frank Taylor of the *Daily Mirror*, survived and he was to spend nearly a year in hospital. And Matt Busby, the father to his young stars who had been christened the Busby Babes, fought to live after the multiple injuries he had sustained in the accident.

Such are the facts of a disaster paralleled in football terms only by the crash at Superga in 1949 which wiped out the Italian League Champions, Torino, as they were flying home from a game in Lisbon. But the facts tell little of the story, for Manchester United were more than a football team – they were, and have remained, an ideal. In 1958 they carried with them the hopes of British football, which had been dealt so many blows throughout that decade in the World Cups of 1950 and 1954 and by the mighty Hungarians at Wembley and in Budapest in 1953 and 1954. England's prospects for the 1958 World Cup perished on that runway in Munich.

United had won the League in 1956 and 1957. They were the first English club side to seriously challenge in Europe, reaching the semi-final of the European Cup in 1957. They had reached the same stage of the 1958 tournament by the draw they had obtained in Belgrade, from where they were returning when they landed at Munich. In 1957 they had only been stopped by the might of Real Madrid. Busby had said afterwards, 'Real were superior only in experience, and we shall soon have that.' That same year United almost became the first side in the 20th century to complete the League and Cup double. After winning the League, they lost the Cup Final 2–1 to Aston Villa only after playing the last 84 minutes without the injured Wood. In 1958 they could easily have won all three competitions.

Football writer James Wilson wrote shortly after the crash, 'Only Arsenal at their height could have rivalled this Manchester United. But even they had their weaknesses. Recently at Highbury there was no apparent weakness in the Manchester side. Moreover, one would not have expected them to reach their best for another year or two.'

The United side appeared to be coming to a spectacular peak at the beginning of 1958. On January 18, the pre-Munich side played their last home game, defeating Bolton Wanderers 7–2. On February 1 came their last ever game in England – a 5–4 win at Highbury that has passed into history as a classic, and an epitaph. On February 5 came the last game of all – a 3–3 draw with Red Star of Belgrade that took them one step nearer the European Cup on a 5–4 aggregate. Bobby Charlton scored two of the goals, and it was a happy United party which landed at the Reim Airport in their chartered plane, despite the bad weather. The stop was for refuelling.

One man not on the plane was Jimmy Murphy, Matt Busby's assistant manager. He was also in charge of the full Wales international side and, the previous evening, had been with that team when they had beaten Israel 2–0 in Cardiff in a World Cup qualifying game. As he said at the time, he would have preferred to be in Belgrade.

The news of the tragedy was broken to him the following day by Matt Busby's secretary. 'My feet stopped, so did my heart,' said Murphy afterwards. Only gradually did it dawn on him that the responsibility for keeping the club going was solely his. He flew to Munich, where Busby whispered 'Keep the flag flying.' Murphy looked at the situation in the hospital with horror. Seven of his players were dead. Duncan Edwards, who fought his fatal injuries with his prodigious strength for a fortnight, was dying. Two more would never play again. Busby battled for life in an oxygen tent. Others like Charlton, Denis Viollet, Ray Wood, Ken Morgans, and Albert Scanlon were out of football for at least several weeks. Only right-back Bill Foulkes and the Irish goalkeeper Harry Gregg had escaped uninjured. And there was no club coach, no trainer, no secretary. Murphy was alone.

As he returned from Bavaria on the Rheingold Express, his problem was not so much to win the next match, but simply to find a team at all. Murphy says he sat numb and dumb while the wheels of the train drummed out 'Where do you find the players? Where do you find the players?' He had Gregg and Foulkes with him, but they were showing signs of panic and claustrophobia, especially when the train braked sharply. They had seen the survivors the day after the crash in hospital, but it was not until they asked to see the others that it had dawned on them that some of their friends and colleagues were dead.

The fixture on Saturday February 8 was naturally postponed. That day the snow came to Britain, as an added reminder of the tragedy; all over the country where matches could take place there was unanimous mourning. Black-armbands were worn; a two-minute silence was observed even by crowds at other sporting occasions; at some grounds, the spectators and the players joined in the singing of Abide With Me. There followed too the awful trappings of a national catastrophe – messages of condolence from world leaders, countless offers of help, and later a memorial service.

Amid this atmosphere of heartbreaking sadness and overwhelming sympathy, Jimmy Murphy had to stop the snowball of emotion before the club was crushed under its weight. He had to find a team. He had to put Manchester United on to the field of play again. He had to show that life at Old Trafford could go on. United were due to meet Sheffield Wednesday in the fifth round of the FA Cup the following Saturday, the 15th; this game, too, had to be put back, but Murphy and the FA agreed to stage the game the following Wednesday.

So Murphy had ten days to find a side; ten days to fill the red shirts. Joe Armstrong, the chief scout, drew up a list of players. As Murphy said, it looked as though it would have to be a team of schoolboys. Liverpool and Nottingham Forest were among the clubs who offered players, but Murphy was generally reluctant to buy. Rushed decisions were likely to be wrong decisions, and hoping against hope that Busby would be able to take up the reins again Murphy did not want his manager to come back to even greater problems than existed already.

In the middle of the quest for the side came the memorial service for those lost. On Monday the 17th it was held at St Martin's-in-the-Fields; there was later a service at Old Trafford itself. In London the Bishop of Chester apositely summed up the status of the club and in doing so emphasised the despair of the tragedy. He said: '... during the last ten years under the genius of Matt Busby, young men have not only been trained to a high standard of technical efficiency but they have also been inspired with a loyalty to the club and to the game which has been a pattern for the best that men can achieve. This character has brought the team to the highest places of the game in the country. It has also made the name of Manchester United a household word. It has also given the team an opportunity of travelling to many foreign countries and there, in addition to playing good football, they have proved themselves fine ambassadors on the football ground and off it.

'When we remember that during the season a million people each week in this country watch professional football, we can appreciate the responsibility which is laid upon these young players. They are admired, idolised, glamorised, imitated. They set a standard which, perhaps unseen, certainly leaves its mark on the moral standards of our society. They have a responsibility not only to play efficiently but to play well, and it is because Manchester United have acquitted themselves so splendidly in the wider as well as the ultimate discharge of their duty that the team has become a byword for those who play a good game wherever football is played.'

Two days after the service, Sheffield Wednesday were to visit Old Trafford. By the morning of the match Murphy had bought just one new player, Ernie Taylor, the veteran inside-forward who had already won Cup-winners' medals with Newcastle United in 1951 and Blackpool two years later; he cost Manchester United £8000. But Murphy knew that his young side would definitely need a strong man, and he remembered the impressive performance given by the robust Aston Villa wing-half Stan Crowther in the 1957 Cup Final against United. Villa agreed to sell but there was a major snag. Crowther had played for Villa in the third round of the competition and was thus Cup-tied. Murphy applied for special permission to play him against Wednesday, but had to wait for a reply from the Football Association. It was not granted until the afternoon of the game, and Murphy completed the transfer in a Manchester hotel just 54 minutes from the kick-off; Villa received £24,000 for the deal.

The official match programme had gone to press with 11 blank spaces under the heading of 'United team', and fans were already setting off from all over the North on their pilgrimage to Old Trafford when Murphy sat down with his team sheet. Gregg was beginning to come round from the mental shock of his ordeal (he and Foulkes had helped pull the injured from the wreckage) and he was fit to go in goal. Foulkes was still shaken but his experience was vital, and Murphy wrote his name on the sheet alongside number two. Taylor and Crowther were the other straightforward selections.

Ian Greaves had played three first-team matches the previous season as Foulkes' full-back partner, so he became the fifth selection. Freddie Goodwin, a shy young reserve, was slotted into the left-half position. The number seven shirt went to Colin Webster, a Welsh international, but he had little knowledge of first-team football.

That was the end of Murphy's experience. Ronnie Cope, a youngster learning his trade in the third team, took the vital centre-half position. Alex Dawson, then an unknown 18-year old, went in at centre-forward. Another teenager, Mark Pearson, was put in alongside Dawson at inside-left. That filled ten places, but with David Pegg dead and other wingmen Berry, Morgans, and Scanlon lying in the Munich hospital, there was no left-winger and no possibility of finding one. Murphy, in his boldest gamble, went to the other end of his 'A' team and gave the job to natural right-back Shay Brennan. It appeared an odd choice, but it paid quite dramatic dividends.

Sheffield Wednesday were in trouble at the foot of the First Division table, and indeed were later relegated without winning a single away match in the League, but the team they brought to Old Trafford had just what United had not got – plenty of experience. Redfern Froggatt, their inside-left, had won four England caps in the early 1950s. Albert Quixall, the other inside-forward, was also an international, a player as eye-catching for his sweet skills as for his crop of blond hair, and a player who was later to become part of the rebuilding of United. Two other young men, Peter Swan and Tony Kay, were also destined to play for their country.

The atmosphere at the ground was astonishing. Roy Perrot in the following day's Manchester *Guardian* described it thus, 'Outside the ground thousands of people waited . . . hoping for a slim chance of a ticket, even at ten times the face value . . . and when they could not get one were apparently satisfied to hang around listening to the sound of soccer history . . .'

United's makeshift 11 were cheered and encouraged at every

touch of the ball. The opposition happened to be Sheffield Wednesday, but it could have been the Brazilian national side or 11 men from Mars for all the difference it would have made. And the hysteria of the crowd was rewarded when Brennan, the most makeshift of the side, gave an inspired performance though totally out of position on the left wing.

His memorable evening began when he took a corner-kick, surely something he was not accustomed to do during his defensive duties in the third team. The ball curled in towards the goal and defeated every attempt by attacker and defender to make contact as though fate was, in a minute way, trying to make up for the wretched blow it had dealt the club. United led to a tumultuous reception from a crowd which did not know whether to cheer or cry.

Brennan had not finished. As the young 'Reds' ran relentlessly for possession, substituting energy for experience, Ernie Taylor prowled the midfield bringing order with shrewd passing and knowing advice; the players, many of whom were around half his age, christened him 'Uncle'. Incredibly, United took hold of the game, and to thunderous acclaim Brennan scored again.

The Sheffield Wednesday players faced an unenviable task; Old Trafford that night was a hard place to retain a clinical professional outlook; for all their loyalty to their own cause it was impossible not to feel sympathy for the stricken Manchester club. And they fell three goals behind when the raw Dawson, battling with all the bravery that was to become his trademark, bustled in to score. The pent-up emotion of the preceding 13 days was all released as United fans roared on their motley squad to a victory that had more in common with fiction than fact.

This was Manchester United's night, the night which breathed new life back into a club that was close to death itself. Wednesday had been there simply to make up the numbers. Bill Foulkes, by now the captain, said afterwards, 'I felt sorry for Sheffield; they were never in the game with a chance. I'm sure that everyone, even their own supporters, were willing us to win. The atmosphere was so electric . . . the crowd was simply hysterical.' In truth the game was not a footballing classic, but all that really mattered was that it was taking place at all. Life was going on. And Wednesday had their revenge soon enough, knocking United out of the Cup in both the 1959–60 and 1960–61 seasons.

There is a belief that United rose phoenix-like from the ashes. But that legend owes everything to their marvellous Cup performances. In the League the rest of the season was little short of disastrous; they took just seven points from their remaining 14 games; but added to the 36 they had acquired before Munich that made a respectable 43, and they finished ninth in the table.

In the Cup the frenetic support produced more magnificent performances. Crowds flocked to see the young side in action. For game after game the gates were closed hours before the kick-off. It was three months of continual hysteria at Old Trafford and elsewhere. In the quarter-final of the Cup they beat West Bromwich 1–0 after a replay, and in the semi-final they disposed of Fulham 5–3, again after a replay. And then there was Wembley – and Busby out of hospital to see it. Charlton and Viollet had recovered, too, and they played instead of Pearson and Brennan of the team that beat Wednesday. The others, Greaves, Goodwin, Cope, Dawson, and Webster, had come through their instant apprenticeship.

Their opponents were Bolton, the same Bolton crushed so convincingly just before Munich. Poor Bolton. Five years earlier the whole country had been willing Stanley Matthews to get his winners' medal in a classic final; that Blackpool side had included Ernie Taylor, who was now to face them again. And now possibly even their own supporters would not have minded had the Cup ended up down the road at Old Trafford. But it was not to be. The fairytale run had been based on emotion, and that was not enough to discourage Nat Lofthouse and, frankly, the better side from winning 2–0.

It took ten years to come anywhere near laying the ghost of Munich when, on a balmy night at Wembley, United became the first English club to win the European Cup. Foulkes was still in the team and Charlton, now the captain, scored two goals just as he had a decade before in Belgrade. Eventually, in 1963, the club received a ridiculous £35,000 compensation for their loss, but by then Busby was building another great side and memories of that night in Manchester were beginning to fade. But it continues to live in the words of the Manchester *Guardian*:

'At the final whistle the crowd moved like a sea under the floodlights, shaking with their own cheers. They will almost have heard that in Munich. And as the triumphant crowd swept homewards, whole families in the same little streets around the ground stood on their doorsteps asking 'Who won? Who scored? What were they like?'' over and over again until they were finally convinced that Old Trafford was back in business.'

THE GLORIOUS DEFEAT

The story of Northern Ireland's tilt at the World Cup

No country in the history of world soccer earned such glory from ultimate defeat as we did.' Peter Doherty, manager of Northern Ireland during a remarkable two weeks in June 1958, spoke with little overstatement. The tiny province with practically no history of international football competition outside its regular sorties with England, Scotland, and Wales had produced a side which had no right to be present at the final stages of a World Cup, yet had tilted, if not quite overturned the balance of power at the top.

The fable was no overnight sensation. Rather it had its beginnings in a blending of talents some years earlier. Peter Doherty appeared to possess only half the attributes of an international manager when his appointment was announced in the mid-1950s, Unquestionably his playing record provided sufficient stature; as an inside-forward with Blackpool, Manchester City, Derby County, Huddersfield Town, and Doncaster Rovers, his flair as a fashioner and finisher of chances made him an outstanding performer. And he represented his country 16 times before and after World War II.

But with his mop of red hair, he looked a rebel – and he was. Proud, and a passionate critic of the exploitation of footballers, he continually stood up against the establishment. His tongue, with all its Irish fluency, often harangued the authorities, which explained his regular movement from one club to another. His eventual elevation to the managership of Northern Ireland seemed certain to create new controversy.

Yet above all, Doherty understood the game, and gave it more thought than many of his contemporaries. And in his squad of players he found men who were also exceptions to the prevalent lack of tactical thinking of the day. Danny Blanchflower was cast in Doherty's image, a player of imagination and awareness; more than that he shared his manager's independence of thought. He had been too independent for Barnsley and Aston Villa, but Tottenham Hotspur suited his style, though his belief in making policy changes on the pitch was to cost him the captaincy of the London club for a while.

Jimmy McIlroy had first put on the green number 10 shirt of Northern Ireland only a year after Doherty himself had pulled it off for the last time. He proved a worthy successor, an inside-forward of perception who similarly believed that strategy and planning were meaningful factors in the way that the game was played. Together Doherty, Blanchflower, and McIlroy formed a triumvirate which came to be the foundation of World Cup heroism.

Not many Irishmen had smiling eyes when the draw for the qualifying group paired them with Italy and Portugal, with the prize for the winner being a place in the last 16 in Sweden. But Doherty's side eliminated the challenge of the Portuguese by drawing 1–1 in Lisbon and beating them in Belfast by three clear goals. Between these two games a courageous performance in Rome had resulted in a 1–0 defeat at the hands of the Italians, but Italy still had to be beaten at home.

For all the cohesion Doherty's leadership was bringing, Ireland had won only one of their last ten games in the Home International Championship – no kind of record with which to disturb the confidence of the experienced Italians. But one month before the return leg was due to be played, they received an injection of confidence from an amazing source. Northern Ireland had not beaten England for 30 years; they had never won at Wembley. Yet Doherty and Blanchflower plotted a victory that had more than a sweet immediacy; it steered the side on to a World Cup course.

The Irish tactical thinking recognised that the game would be decided in midfield, where England possessed a player of the highest calibre in Johnny Haynes. As the favourites swarmed forward with Haynes at the hub of every attack, it looked as

The moment he'd been waiting for. The Queen, flanked by the Duke of Edinburgh and Stanley Rous, presents Stanley Matthews with his well-deserved FA Cup-winners' medal after the 1953 final against Bolton Wanderers.

Manchester United in 1957 – a year before the tragic air crash in Munich.

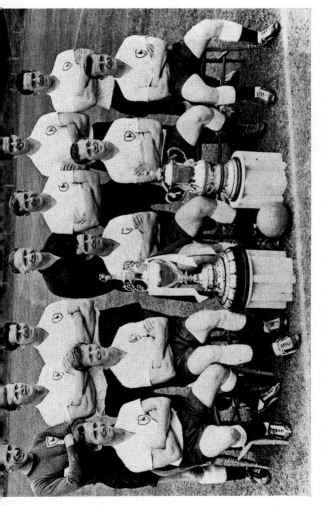

The first modern double winners – Spurs at the end of the 1960-61 season. Pictured (left to right from back) are: Brown, Baker, Henry, Nicholson, Blanchflower, Norman, Mackay, Jones, White, Smith, Allen, Dyson.

The 1973 FA Cup final between Leeds and Sunderland was one of the most sensational of post-war days, with the underdogs winning in a welter of emotion. Bobby Kerr, Sunderland's young captain, sits astride Dennis Tueart for the traditional photographs, and scorer Ian Porterfield is second from the right.

though the pre-planning had been misguided. But Blanch-flower, a general at the front, created instant re-organisation. By squeezing Haynes into a corridor near the touchline, Blanchflower limited his options. By urging McIlroy and left-half Bertie Peacock into resolute marking he restricted England's alternative build-up. Three-two was the margin of a victory, which in every way was tactical.

But there followed no easy route to qualification for the World Cup finals. When Italy came to Belfast in December 1957, so did the fog – not enough to prevent a match, but enough to delay the arrival of the Hungarian referee, Istvan Zsolt. Without the appropriate officials, any game played could only be a friendly, though the 90 minutes offered by the two teams was far from that. Ill-temper on the pitch provoked a reaction in the crowd, some of whom were so incensed that they stormed the playing area. The result – a 2–2 draw – was far from irrelevant, but the atmosphere may have inhibited the Italians when the official match was played five weeks later. Then, in a considerably more controlled atmosphere, Ireland won 2–1 with goals from McIlroy and the versatile Wilbur Cush.

That match proved to be the last international for Jackie Blanchflower, brother of Danny, whose steadiness at centre-half had contributed greatly to the efficiency of the team. Blanchflower, like the first-choice goalkeeper Harry Gregg, travelled to Belgrade with Manchester United and was seriously injured in the tragedy of the Munich airfield on the return journey. Gregg, a lucky survivor, was soon back in action, but Blanchflower never played again.

No automatic replacement at centre-half had been found when the Irish party set off for Sweden towards the end of May 1958. Their arrival at their camp close by the town of Halm-stad caused barely a ripple of interest. Brazil, holders West Germany, Hungary, Russia and England – these were the teams of interest to the media. Northern Ireland were even a bit of a nuisance – after all, they had eliminated Italy, who would have been a much bigger draw.

But the Irish players had their own thoughts. 'We feared no

one,' remembered Peter Doherty. 'We had been thrilled to qualify. That was an achievement in itself. But we weren't just going for the ride. The players had a tremendous will to win, and we were lucky enough to have four world class players in our squad. Though the rest of the lads were really only ordinary League men, they responded because we were organised and we had character.'

Doherty's house rules at the training headquarters were disciplined: 'I was really strict with the players. I imposed curfews and watched them closely in training so that they really worked. For example, I wouldn't let them train in twos, because they can chatter and perhaps make a pact to take it easy. But there was no problem. We had built up a great respect for each other. It was a family atmosphere.'

The presence of England, Scotland, and Wales in the final 16 deflected even the domestic limelight away from Ireland as they opened their programme in Group One against Czechoslovakia, who were expected to provide a significant threat to the favourites. The centre-half problem had not been resolved, so Doherty asked his regular right-back, Willie Cunningham of Leicester City, to play there for the first time in an international. Doherty had also searched through his limited resources to find a goalscoring centre-forward, and in desperation chose a raw youngster to lead the line – Derek Dougan, then with Portsmouth.

Cunningham met with considerably more success than Dougan against Czechoslovakia. Doherty's side defended with skill and organisation, helped by Blanchflower, who restricted his forward movements from right-half. And it was Ireland who pilfered the game's only goal. There was no one in the party with a more 'Irish' playing style than Wilbur Cush. Standing just 5ft 5ins tall, he had already played in the centre of his country's defence, and also that of Leeds United – astounding tall strikers by winning the ball in the air with huge leaps. Now, from his role as an inside-forward, he popped up to score in a breakaway attack.

The euphoria was short-lived. Three days later, anti-climax. Argentina had lost 3–1 to West Germany while Ireland were

82

winning, and they recalled their experienced players, amongst them a 40-year-old, inside-left Labruna. Perhaps the Irish were psychologically undone by the appearance of several tubby, ageing opponents. They had the boost of an early goal from the rampaging power of left-winger Peter McParland, but slumped to a 3-1 defeat. With West Germany drawing with the Czechs, the odds against Ireland qualifying lengthened considerably.

Four days later they had barely shortened, despite a marvellously courageous draw against the holders, West Germany. Doherty still sought desperately for a striker – Fay Coyle, a Nottingham Forest reserve, had played against Argentina – and chose Tommy Casey, a wing-half by background, to wear the number nine shirt. But he still had the drive of McParland at his disposal, and it was the aggressive winger who took the game to the Germans.

He shot Ireland into a shock lead, only for Helmut Rahn, the giant of the 1954 final, to equalise two minutes later. In the second half McParland found the net again, but 11 minutes from Ireland's qualification for the quarter-finals, West Germany fashioned another equaliser, this time from a new hero, the young Uwe Seeler. In between the goals, Harry Gregg had performed miracles to thwart the holders, but in doing so had given an ankle a violent twist.

Ireland now had three points. So too had Czechoslovakia, who slaughtered the ageing Argentinians 6-1. So there had to be a play-off to decide who accompanied West Germany into the quarter-finals. And the Czechs, with their better goal average needed only to draw. Gregg, who could move only with the help of a stick, could not play, and on top of that setback the party had become beset with travel problems.

The play-off was to take place in Malmö, where Ireland had played West Germany, but no accommodation could be found for the Irish players, who had to traipse the 100 miles back to Halmstad and then return two days later for the match. But this inconvenience did not prevent the one concession in the Doherty code of discipline. 'I gave them a free night after each game. I told them to enjoy themselves, and I didn't want to see them but I didn't want them to see the legislators either. That was the only freedom they had.'

As well as Gregg, the side for the play-off also lacked the unfit Tommy Casey. Jackie Scott of Grimsby became the fourth man to wear the centre-forward's jersey. Yet, because he was a natural winger, he was given a role along the touch-lines with the more physical McParland leading the attack in the centre. Doherty made no other changes, and nine of the eleven looked tired and tense as they lined up against the Czechs for their fourth tilt at windmills inside nine days.

They could hardly have expected a worse start. Within a minute Norman Uprichard, Gregg's replacement, sustained an ankle injury remarkably similar to that of the first-choice 'keeper. After a quarter of an hour of tense play, his lack of mobility was a handicap when he couldn't extricate himself from no-man's land as a ball was played into his goalmouth. Zikan, the outside-left, headed the cross past him. Even the proudest Irish heads on the field drooped slightly.

But their confidence had not totally deserted them. As the referee inspected his watch to count down the final seconds of the first half, Billy Bingham's break on the right created a chance for Cush. As the moments ticked away, the diminutive inside-forward fired at goal. A defender blocked it. He stabbed at the rebound, and again a Czech leg stopped the shot. A third time Cush tried before deflecting the ball into the path of McParland. His drive had hardly settled in the back of the net before the whistle was blown for the interval.

The ten-minute break seemed barely sufficient for the desperately needed recharging of energies, and yet in the second period even greater demands were to be placed on the fitness and character of the Irishmen. In the first dangerous Czech raid of the half, Uprichard flung himself to keep out a shot from Dvorak so fierce that the goalkeeper's hand was pinned against the goalpost, and a bone broken. Uprichard's face contorted with agony on every subsequent contact with the ball.

On one such occasion only minutes later, his throbbing hands could not wholly grasp another shot, and the ball rolled dangerously loose. Bertie Peacock and Zikan both flung themselves at it as in blind gallantry Uprichard dived again. Peacock bore the brunt of the crunch and his knee collapsed under the strain. Already cruelly under the handicap of Uprichard's injury, Northern Ireland now had their left-half limping on the left wing.

Yet Czechoslovakia could not kill off their wounded opponents. Doherty's insistence on character and discipline could not have been put to any greater test. And somehow, with Blanchflower outstanding, the Irish reached the temporary sanctuary of full-time with the score still 1–1.

The conversation during the short respite before extra-time naturally centred on Uprichard. Doherty looked at the injury and advised him to come off and go for an immediate X-Ray. Uprichard refused to turn his back on his colleagues, but suggested that he should play on the field with someone else taking over in goal. Blanchflower's persuasive tongue urged him to stay put. And Blanchflower had his way.

Doherty was still conscious that a gallant draw would not be enough, that goal average would go against him. He turned towards the group of Czechs and exhorted his players: 'We are tired, but look at them. They are a lot tireder!' At the same time Bingham added his own brand of kidology by going through a series of exercises with the enthusiasm of a man who had not played for a week rather than one playing his fourth game in nine days.

And when the game restarted in the gathering gloom, it was Ireland who surged into the attack. Now the Czechs had to defend in desperation, and they could only survive for ten minutes. Then Blanchflower carefully placed the ball for a free-kick and looked goalwards. He saw McParland and drove the ball towards the tall forward, and his own fatigue had not detracted from his accuracy. Nor had McParland's quality of finishing been diminished, and he turned the ball into the Czech goal. As McParland was engulfed, 11 Czech mouths hung open in disbelief.

Still 20 minutes remained. Those loyal fans who had come from Ulster to Sweden bellowed out chours upon chorus of *When Irish Eyes Are Smiling*. Doherty, down on the touchline, bellowed his own battle-cries. Irish officials turned their backs on the play unable to cope with the strain of watching. Finally the Czechs yielded to frustration. Their right-half Bubernik ran to the referee to complain about a push in his back going unpunished, and when his protestations fell on deaf ears he spat at the official, who duly sent him off.

Now the inequality had lessened. A fact emphasised by the hobbling Peacock when he turned in a pass from Scott. But an offside flag ruled out the score, and robbed the game of one further romantic twist. And still Czechoslovakia, now desperately aware of an impending exit from the competition, drove forward in search of an equaliser. And yet again aching Irish legs barred their way.

Then the coveted victory was theirs. As the supporters and officials danced in joy, Blanchflower, whose brain had never lost its sharp edge in the drama, asked one more task of his side – a round of applause for the Czechs. Then it was the celebration of the dressing-room. An upsurge of emotion before Doherty began to assess the cost of victory.

Now he had no goalkeepers and barely ten fit outfield players. Uprichard's wrist was put straight into plaster while Gregg still moved with heavy reliance on his stick, and now there was still more travelling to interfere with the treatment of the afflicted.

On the night of the match, Tuesday June 17, the players cheerfully sang their way back to base. The following day, only 24 hours prior to the quarter-final against France, they journeyed for ten hours across Sweden to Norrköping, and they did not arrive at their hotel until the small hours of the very morning of the match. Doherty later admitted that he had been wrong in the way that he had scheduled the travelling.

There had been little proper rest. Tommy Casey, still sore from the West Germany match, was selected to play instead of Peacock. Gregg had to play in goal and Doherty remembered his last psychological throw of the dice: 'I was worried that we should give the wrong impression, arriving with one goalkeeper in plaster and the other on a stick. So I told Gerry Morgan, my trainer, to sneak up on Harry Gregg and steal his stick. But he never got it. Gregg never let it out of his sight. And sure enough he turned up at the ground to play in a World Cup quarter-final on a stick!'

With England and Scotland already out, Ireland, together with Wales, who played and lost gallantly to Brazil in their quarter-final, carried the hopes of Britain. But this time the task was too much. France beat them by four clear goals.

And in the quiet of that loser's dressing room, the captain of the men Doherty described as the greatest set of lads he had ever known broke the silence. Danny Blanchflower lifted his gaze from the floor and said: 'Never mind, what we've done might never happen again.'

A MATCH TO REMEMBER

The story of the fifth European Cup final

When those who preserve records of our society to be discovered by future generations decide to leave a relic of football, they must consult experts on the preservation of celluloid. For there could be no finer testimony to everything that is good in the game than a 90-minute film of the 1960 European Cup final – a classic dish served up by Real Madrid and Eintracht Frankfurt.

The setting of Glasgow's vast Hampden Park enabled almost 130,000 lucky spectators to witness a match of technical perfection. Those present paid a then record £55,000 to see the game and the many thousands of Scots, for all their traditional penny-pinching philosophies, must have felt that they had had supreme value for their money.

The ten-goal fiesta also emphasised the gulf between these top sides and the best that Britain had to offer in 1960. The Scottish audience were only too well aware that Eintracht had outclassed Rangers, the pride of Glasgow, in the semi-final. In Frankfurt, they had crushed Scotland's champions 6–1, and this despite an indifferent record in the German League; the second leg brought further disasters as Eintracht stunned the Ibrox Park crowd by winning 6–3 and setting statisticians thumbing the records books to find out when, if ever, a team had put 12 goals past Rangers in two matches.

Real Madrid's semi-final form had also spelt out the vast failings in British football. They beat Barcelona 6–2 on aggregate and Real's Spanish rivals had devastated the hopes of the Football League champions, Wolverhampton Wanderers. Wolves had fallen by four clear goals in Barcelona and saved neither the tie nor face when they lost 5–2 at Molineux. But if

England's star was in decline, Spain's could not have achieved greater ascendancy.

Real and Eintracht met in the fifth European Cup final and at that time only the name of Real Madrid appeared on the trophy. In 1956 they had beaten Rheims 4–3 in the first final in Paris, the following year Fiorentina were their victims in Madrid; in 1958 another Italian side, AC Milan, fell in the Heysel Stadium in Brussels; and Real won their fourth title in 1959 by again beating Rheims, this time in Stuttgart.

The Real Chairman, Don Santiago Bernabeu, had lifted a club which in the early 1950s had average gates of 15,000 to one which was the wealthiest in Spain, and he spent the profits wisely on star players. Undoubtedly his greatest acquisition was the Argentinian Alfredo di Stefano, who arrived from South America with the reputation of being an above average goalscoring centre-forward. But in Spain his game matured dramatically. Without losing any of his flair in front of goal he developed into the focal point of the team – a player of immense energy who covered the entire pitch in Real's cause, who defended willingly, and who possessed such vision that he engineered events with disarming ease. Di Stefano was the complete general.

But perhaps Real's greatest feat had been to blend di Stefan's gifts with those of the great Hungarian exile, Ferenc Puskas. Initially it had been an uneasy marriage. Puskas, too, had been used to generaliship and for a while Real had stammered like an army led by two conflicting officers of equal rank. But the Hungarian found the answer when, towards the end of their first season together, the two star forwards were neck and neck at the top of the Real's goalscoring lists; Puskas, with a simple chance of a goal, opted to pass to di Stefano who scored, and from that moment he was accepted by the Argentinian.

Nor were Real a two-man team. The attack was given width by the fleet-of-foot Francisco Gento who played in all Real's European finals in the 1950s, survived the next decade, and played in the Real side which lost the 1970–71 Cup-Winners' Cup final to Chelsea. Another regular Spanish international was the perceptive inside-forward Luis Del Sol, and the five-man attack to meet Eintracht was completed by the Brazilian winger, Canario.

Though the defence was often forgotten in the praise that was heaped upon the forward line, two foreigners – Dominguez, who had kept goal for Argentina, and Santamaria, who had represented Uruguay in the 1954 World Cup – were as much masters of their own less thrilling crafts as di Stefano and Puskas. Marquitos, the right-back, had played in the finals of 1956 and 1957 while Zarraga, another consistent defender was, like di Stefano and Gento, going for a nap hand of winners' medals.

On paper Eintracht had no such roll of honour. None of their side had won a German cap that season, but trainer Paul Osswald had built a strong side with pace in its attack around two experienced linkmen, Richard Kress and Alfred Pfaff, both in their mid-30s and both of whom had joined the club when its name was totally unknown outside Germany. As they had shown against Rangers, their forwards carried a goalscoring threat, an attack led with gusto by an enthusiastic youngster, Erwin Stein.

And to the surprise of the huge crowd, massed tightly together on the steep banks of Hampden Park, it was the attack led by Stein rather than that led by di Stefano that began the more impressively. Erich Meier, another forward with acceleration to trouble defenders and a willingness to use it, sent in a curving shot which Dominguez misjudged and the ball rebounded from the cross bar. Del Sol exhibited the first true flash of class from Real with some deft footwork which might have brought a goal but for an alert stop by Loy, but Eintracht were responding to the promptings of Pfaff. For the first quarter of an hour the Germans scoffed at those who had completely written off their chances.

And after 18 minutes the scoreline reflected their good start. Stein's speed created the chance. Moving wide he beat two defenders in a powerful run down the right touchline. The burst totally upset the balance in the Real rearguard and when Stein cut the ball back, no white-shirted defender picked up Kress as he sprinted in at the near post. A neatly struck volley turned the ball into the narrow gap between the woodwork and Dominguez's belated dive.

Real reacted immediately to the sting. For all their panache in attack, their's was a reputation founded on a beautiful simplicity in prising open defences, and the equaliser, six minutes after Kress's goal, bore that trademark. The ball was switched to the right flank, to the feet of Canario; the Brazilian winger, who had not adjusted easily to European conditions and who had spent recent months out of the first team, slipped a defender and crossed early and low. Lunging German feet flailed in vain as the ball flew into the path of di Stefano's urgent run; and like an irritated schoolmaster rapping the knuckles of a cheeky pupil, the Argentinian master, now 34 years old, drove past Loy. Eintracht had led for just six minutes.

They remained on equal terms for just half that time. Loy was already beginning to show signs that his nerves were finding the occasion very testing, and he was directly at fault for Real's second goal. The angles were all in the goalkeeper's favour when Canario, just inside the right hand corner of the penalty area, struck for goal right-footed. But Loy, diving to his left, could not cope with the swerve of the low shot and the ball bounced from his arms back into the goal area. It was a situation tailormade for strikers of the poaching ability of Jimmy Greaves, Denis Law, and, of course, Alfredo di Stefano, though the measure of di Stefano's class was that he managed to arrive in such positions although seconds earlier he might have been in his own penalty area or instigating the attack from midfield.

Sure enough, di Stefano had sensed the possibility of such an error and his reactions carried him to the ball ahead of two defenders and Loy who made a death-or-glory lunge to try to rectify his mistake. Di Stefano was one step ahead in movement and in thought and he turned the ball easily into the bottom corner. Real led 2-1 as, understandably, Eintracht struggled to contain the greatest player of the day.

The game now belonged to di Stefano. Stimulated by the vast crowd and the knowledge that millions more were watching the game live on television, he played to the gallery but without the slightest trace of self-indulgence. Whenever Real were in possession he would be the target for his colleagues' passes and whenever di Stefano had the ball there was no respite for Eintracht. The Argentinian's style, combined with his fair thinning hair, had earned him the nickname of the 'Golden Arrow' and in attack after attack Real fired their bow. His colleagues could not fail to respond to such an example.

Loy's goal could not possibly withstand the incessant pressure, and shortly before half-time Real added their third – scored by Puskas. It was as though di Stefano had now allowed those around him to take a hand. Del Sol was the instigator and the Eintracht rearguard, dizzy from its efforts over the preceding 20 minutes, could not contain the inside-right as he dribbled into the penalty area. But they did manage to prevent the Spaniard from getting in a shot, and he switched the ball to Puskas who, near the goalline on the left hand side of the penalty area, also seemed not particularly well placed to score.

But that was a judgement for mere mortals, not for the supernatural skills of Ferenc Puskas. Thicker around the tummy than in his great days in Hungary, he had lost nothing in mobility; nor had the phenomenal power of his shooting diminished. A quick shimmy lost an opponent, and though the angles were all against him he slashed a left-footed thunderbolt past Loy, whose raised arms might well have been in self-protection rather than in a helpless attempt to stop the ball. In coaching terms Loy should never have been beaten from such an angle, but the velocity of such shooting came outside the scope of such manuals.

Puskas would remember better than most the durability of German teams, and at half-time he might have given a moment's reflection to the events of the World Cup final six years earlier. Then Hungary had led by two clear goals only to lose in the second half to Germany, a team which man for man had looked their inferior. But after their first half performance it would take an upset of even greater proportion to prevent Real from winning their fifth European Cup.

In the Eintracht dressing-room they had to try to solve the problems posed by di Stefano and Puskas, but if they concentrated their efforts on stopping these two, the breadth of Real's talent ensured that danger would spring up from another direction. And sure enough early in the second period Real successfully used another route to goal.

This time it was the pace of Gento which ran the German defence ragged. Nine minutes into the second half the right-back Lutz could not quite match the left-winger's electric dash into the penalty area. The defender reached the ball but only at the expense of a nudge on Gento, which looked more like obstruction than an out-and-out push. But the referee instantly indicated his verdict – a penalty – a sentence which, unless Loy could produce some heroics, surely spelt death to any linger-ing expectancy of an Eintracht recovery.

With the kick entrusted to Puskas, Loy's chances were minimal and the Hungarian, as expected, produced the perfect spot-kick. Using his artistic left foot on a mere penalty was rather like Cezanne taking his paintbrush to decorate the front door. But he performed the task with fluency, the low shot sliding inches inside Loy's left-hand post, well away from the goalkeeper's acrobatic gesture.

Soon Gento was on the rampagne again. Del Sol gave mean-ing to yet another Real attack by putting his left-winger in possession. Like a rugby three-quarter he sped for the goal-line, again leaving Lutz blinking in bewilderment. Crossing the ball during such a sprint required the balance and timing of a sure technique, and this was not beyond Gento's talents. Inches short of running the ball out of play he wrapped his left foot around it and pulled it back across the face of the goal. Puskas' instincts had brought him to the edge of the goal area and the cross arrived chest high; instantly adjusting his position he stooped to hammer in a header. Five-one to Real, and Puskas now had a hat-trick to his name, the first to be scored in a European Cup final.

Soon he became the first man to score four in such a final, and the only surprise to the spellbound crowd was that it took him all of ten minutes to get his next goal, so dominating had Real become. With their forwards, all of whom were quite capable of taking on the entire defence single-handed, interchanging positions and interpassing magnetically, the Spanish champions provided a thrilling spectacle, while Eintracht, in the rare moments they were granted possession, still ran forward undaunted in pursuit of scores of their own; never in defence did they resort to cynical and violent methods of solving their problems.

Puskas' fourth goal ended another sustained period of pressure. Zarraga and Puskas took over the play on the left hand side of Real's attack and again they fed Gento. Again his pumping legs took him to the bye-line, though this time the cross was headed clear by a defender. Vidal rather aimlessly drove the ball back and it arrived by chance within the reach of Puskas, though behind him. With one touch of the ball he had it under control and as he turned silkily he already had his left foot cocked ready to fire. From just inside the penalty area the marksmanship was faultless; again Loy had no chance of covering his left hand post and the ball flew, higher this time, just inside it. The crowd, captivated by such magic, bellowed their approval.

Just how their morale coped with such events one will never know, but Eintracht somehow responded with another willing attack – and the gods rewarded their spirit with a splendid goal. The coltish Stein attacked the centre of Real's defence and, faced by two defenders, he veered to the left; no white-shirt moved quickly enough to block his course a second time and he slammed a cross-shot way past Dominguez and inside the junction between far post and crossbar. It was as though he had learned well from the many moments in the game when he had been but a spectator of the march of Madrid. Neither Puskas nor di Stefano had produced a better scoring shot.

Perhaps di Stefano felt that for just one moment an intruder had shown affrontery in taking over his stage, because his retort was to produce *the* moment in a match full of great events. Real restarted and after an exchange of passes the ball was at di Stefano's feet around the half-way aline. After a quick look to assess the possibilities, the 'Golden Arrow' sped at the heart of the Eintracht defence; one or two tentative challenges were brushed aside, others committed the folly of backing off and in seconds he was within 25 yards of goal. Loy by now had plenty of practice of diving to his left and this again was the direction of di Stefano's shot, but again the bullet was accurately fired. It was the perfect individualistic goal from the perfect individualist.

Surprisingly, and to their credit, the tenth and last goal of this extravaganza belonged to Eintracht. Vidal badly misjudged a back pass, and Stein, whose optimism had never faltered, dashed in to capitalise and score his second goal. With 15 minutes still to play the Hampden audience anticipated further excesses at the feast, but though Real played the ball all around the wide pitch with cunning and arrogance they could find no more goals; nor could Eintracht break through again.

Had this been a performance in the theatre there would have been endless curtain calls, so thunderous was the applause at the final whistle. The Scots whose attitude to international football, still some years before Celtic became a European power, rarely extended beyond the patriotism engendered by the clashes between their national team and England, had fallen under the spell of the Spaniards. And they could have stamped and roared no more enthusiastically had it been Rangers and not Real who paraded the trophy to all corners of the ground.

Those who witnessed the game will never forget it however many other football matches they attend. It was the perfect memorial to a great team and a club which had provided the impetus behind the new concept of European club football – for a memorial it turned out to be! After five years of invincibility they were to bow out of the sixth European Cup in the first round, less than six months after the poetry of Hampden Park.

Despite that devastating form they had not retained their League title, losing out on goal average to Barcelona. So Barcelona too qualified for the European Cup and a quirk of the draw paired them with the holders. The first leg in Madrid found Real out of sorts and they could only draw 2–2, though Barcelona needed a last-minute penalty to obtain that result. In Barcelona Real had two goals disallowed and fell two goals behind; Del Sol reduced the deficit five minutes from the end but in a frenetic finish could not quite level the scores. The kings were dead and in this rival Spanish city they were proclaiming new kings.

But Barcelona were never to ascend to the throne; they lost in the 1961 final to Benfica. Nor could Benfica, for all their talented individuals, ever quite match the quality that Real produced in Scotland. Indeed anyone present at Hampden Park would argue that no team has yet matched what they witnessed that day.

TOTT-EN-HAM!
TOTT-EN-HAM!

The story of the first modern 'double'

As time turned the corner into the 1960s, opinion in football was adamant. Winning the Football League Championship and the FA Cup – the 'double' – was akin to walking on water. Mere mortals would drown in the attempt.

That the feat had been twice accomplished, by Preston in 1889 and Aston Villa eight years later was irrelevant; their achievement belonged entirely to those days of fewer fixtures and less intense competition. As the decades rolled by and the pressures increased, the double had been beyond many a great side. Huddersfield Town in the 1920s, Arsenal in the 1930s, Wolves and Manchester United in the 1950s had dominated domestic competition, but had failed to grasp both prizes within the same season.

And the 1960s were no more than a couple of months old when another tilt at the windmill foundered. Wolverhampton Wanderers again struck out for both trophies, and they were more fortunate than others in that rather than falling between the two stools they clung on to the FA Cup. But the other slipped from their grasp when, with the League Championship in their sights, they were not so much beaten as destroyed on their own ground by Tottenham Hotspur.

In fact, Spurs were giving notice of intention. As they returned to London after ending yet another stab at the rainbow, the players reflected on whether the double would ever be achieved, and, still intoxicated by their own display at Molineux, concluded that they might be a better side than any which had failed.

97

Their's was a side not just of talent but also of resolution, a quality which emanated from the top. Their Yorkshire-born manager Bill Nicholson had been with the London club for close on 25 years, first as an inside-forward and then as a defensive wing-half in the side which won the Second Division and First Division Championship in successive years in 1950 and 1951. Later he had graduated to club coach and assistant manager, before in 1958 succeeding Jimmy Anderson as manager; it was a memorable beginning, for Spurs offered a 10-4 beating of Everton as a welcome to the new commander of their ship.

But while Nicholson, dedicated and outwardly dour, tried to put his ideas into practice and assemble a squad of sufficient stature, Spurs struggled. They finished 18th in 1959 as Nicholson sifted through his staff for the right blend, but shortly before the end of that season he made a decision which took a long step in the right direction. He re-appointed Danny Blanchflower as captain.

Blanchflower, an urbane and erudite Irishman, was a gifted, intuitive wing-half, a thinker both off and on the field. He had succeeded Nicholson in the number four shirt at White Hart Lane, though his panache in attack was totally dissimilar to Nicholson's penchant for defence. Blanchflower had been captain before, but for certain club officials his thinking had been too radical. Often a rebel with a cause and occasionally a rebel without one, he had been relieved of his duties three years earlier, even though he remained a highly successful leader of his country. Now, at 33, Nicholson gave him the reins again, and his sense of culture was to leave its imprint on the style of Spurs.

Blanchflower, at £30,000 from Aston Villa in 1954, had been an expensive buy, as had Maurice Norman at £20,000 from Norwich City a year later. Norman had then been a right-back but his 6ft 1in frame had proved even more useful at centre-half, a position in which he was later to represent England. When Nicholson took over, he had other costly signings at his disposal. Bobby Smith, barrel chested and big hearted, and like Nicholson a Yorkshireman, had been moulded by Chelsea into

98

an aggressive centre-forward when Spurs paid £20,000 for him in December 1955, while the club made Cliff Jones the most expensive winger in history when they wrote out a £35,000 cheque to Swansea Town in February 1958.

But money had not bought the blend. Spurs were not a poor club, so Nicholson took his turn to dig into the coffers. He set up a deal with Chelsea that brought a promising young centre-forward, Les Allen, to White Hart Lane, and then converted him to an industrious inside-left of sure touch and with a genuine goalscorer's eye for a chance. He had searched for a goalkeeper and eventually persuaded Dundee to part with Bill Brown, a Scottish international, and it was also in Scotland that he rather fortuitously struck a vein of the purest gold.

Nicholson had in fact turned his gaze to Wales, and he made preparations to sign Mel Charles, the promising younger brother of the supremely talented John. Mel plumped, instead, for Arsenal and Nicholson accepted as second best at the time the purchase of a buccaneering wing-half who had inspired Heart of Midlothian to a succession of Scottish honours. The signature on the transfer forms belonged to Dave Mackay, and his charisma and barnstorming rejection of defeat transformed Spurs from a stylish team into a stylish team of winners.

Mackay also played a part in fitting the last piece of the jigsaw. He and Bill Brown played for Scotland in a 4-0 route of Northern Ireland, who were led as usual by Blanchflower. The three Spurs players returned to London to exhort Nicholson into buying an inside-forward from Falkirk who had masterminded Scotland's win. Blond and waif-like, John White did not fit into Nicholson's image of the player he needed, but once he saw him in action he was convinced. Spurs paid £20,000 for the youngster whose name was largely unknown outside his home country, but Blanchflower has always insisted that White's skills made that transaction 'barefaced robbery'.

Peter Baker, the Hampstead-born defender, had succeeded Alf Ramsey with much of his predecessor's consistency and another of Spurs' own products, Ron Henry, had become a strong-tackling left-back. Henry had been introduced to the club by an army pal of his, Terry Dyson, and Dyson too had impressed Nicholson with the way he had overcome his physical disadvantages.

At 5ft 3in and 9½ stone, he looked every inch a jockey, and it was no surprise to discover that his father had been in that profession, but his speed and bravery in the penalty area won him a place in front of the Welsh international winger Terry Medwin.

After their crushing win at Molineux, Spurs had finished third in the league, one point behind the Cup Winners, who had lost the other half of their double to Burnley by a single point. Nicholson's side looked a good bet for the 1960-61 League title, or the FA Cup, but not both; only fools would bet on the double – or those with prophetic vision!

Any punter with money on Tottenham to win the Championship was mentally spending his winnings before the end of September, for in the League Spurs made an unprecedented start. But not without a battle . . . with themselves. They were at full strength for their opening game, ironically a home match with Everton, a repeat of Nicholson's baptismal fixture two seaons earlier. The teamsheet read: Brown, Baker, Henry, Blanchflower, Norman, Mackay, Jones, White, Smith, Allen, Dyson.

For 85 minutes the flair produced no reward. At times the attack flowed with precision and beauty, as if there were no limits to what they could achieve. But no goals and intermittent stammerings of indecision suggested that the sharpest cutting edge was again missing. But Blanchflower continued to probe with brain and boot, and alongside Mackay, bawling and cajolling, drove his team mates forward.

With five minutes remaining Allen did not wait for a referee's whistle when Smith appeared to be fouled in the Everton penalty area; he belted the ball into the net and a spell was broken. Three minutes later White lifted a clipped pass into the path of Smith and the willing centre-forward scored the second. It was the first of 11 straight wins.

Though missing the injured Jones, Spurs travelled to Blackpool and won 3-1. A second away win came at Blackburn

4-1, and then a Bobby Smith hat-trick completed the double over Blackpool. The centre-forward added two more in a 4-1 thrashing of Manchester United at White Hart Lane, and by now he had set a new club scoring record. Home and away wins followed over Bolton and the sweet filling to the sandwich of these two victories was a triumphant visit to Highbury.

Smith was now injured, but it took only 12 minutes for his deputy, the young Frank Saul, to register his first League goal. Dyson put the visitors two in front before Spurs had to exhibit the extent of their new resillience when Herd and Ward levelled the scores. In the recent past the odds would have been on an Arsenal win but this time Allen, just seven minutes from time, shot the decider.

They saw out September with a 2-1 win at Leicester and a 6-2 extravaganza at home to Aston Villa, and then on October 1 retraced that journey to Molineux. This time the victory resembled a rout, Spurs triumphing with goals from Blanch-flower, Jones, Allen, and Dyson without reply. Eleven games had been played and they had 22 points. Just ten goals had been conceded while Spurs had amassed 36, 13 of them to Smith.

Winning is an exquisite habit, but the hundred per cent record built pressures of its own, and many of the players were relieved when Manchester City earned a 1-1 draw on a Monday night at White Hart Lane. And they picked up their routine with gusto, thrashing Forest 4-0 at the City Ground, winning 4-3 at St James Park, Newcastle, and comfortably defeating Cardiff and Fulham at home. Now Spurs boasted 31 points from 16 League games, and the remainder trailed them helplessly.

Sheffield Wednesday had given early evidence of their own consistency, and at Hillsborough on November 12 Tottenham lost their unbeaten record, the protection of which had also added an unnecessary strain. The relief bubbled out of the players as they travelled back to London, beaten 2-1 in a frenetic game inside a packed ground.

But Wednesday and the other challengers had to wait for any more signs of faltering steps; in the next game the League leaders walloped Birmingham 6–0. And by the halfway mark in the season they had dropped just one more point and that in a classic encounter at White Hart Lane with the defending champions. Spurs tore into Burnley with the venom of men with a message to impart. Jones, twice, Norman and Mackay scored goals which pronounced the end of a reign. But from four in arrears Burnley unveiled their own colours and Jimmy McIlroy's delicious promptings announced to the audience that Northern Ireland had produced more than one creative general. Jimmy Robson, Ray Pointer, and John Connelly, twice, responded to McIlroy's inspiration and the 4–4 draw remains one of the most exhilarating games ever staged at White Hart Lane.

The return with Everton at Goodison marked the start of the inward half of the season, and the Tottenham cockerel continued to crow. A 3–1 win was followed by a Christmas double over West Ham, and a New Year's Eve thrashing of Blackburn Rovers 5–2. But with the advent of 1961 the first cracks appeared in their invincibility. There were reasons. Jones was injured again and would miss most of the January games: White had lost some of his incisiveness on the heavy grounds; even the ebullient Mackay was feeling the pace from the massive amount of work he undertook for himself. It needed all Blanchflower's helmsmanship and Nicholson's reading of the conditions to keep on course.

The FA Cup provided a new challenge, and sufficient inspiration, particularly in a pair of easy ties, but their League form was suffering. Spurs' visit to Manchester United had to be re-arranged for a Monday night because of fog on the Saturday, and with reserves Ken Barton and John Smith in their line-up, Tottenham were beaten even though goalkeeper Harry Gregg was injured and swapped jerseys with forward Alex Dawson. In front of a 65,000 crowd, Stiles and Pearson scored for United while Spurs could not embarrass Dawson and for the first time in the season failed to score.

Other lapses followed and a 12-point lead over Sheffield Wednesday was whittled away. Leicester inflicted a third defeat when they sensationally won 3–2 at White Hart Lane.

Wolves, too, came to London and obtained a draw. And then in March came two terrible reverses, a 3–2 defeat at Ninian Park by an average Cardiff City and a 2–1 home beating by Newcastle who were to be relegated at the end of the season; it was of little consolation that on chances Tottenham should have reached double figures. Their lead at the top of the table dropped to three points.

Though they continued to progress in the Cup, as Easter approached no one at White Hart Lane needed reminding that their performances at the previous year's festival had dissolved their hopes of the championship. The Easter programme read Chelsea at home on Good Friday and away on Easter Monday with a home game against Preston on the Saturday. The three games yielded maximum fruit and the corner was turned.

When Sheffield Wednesday came to White Hart Lane on April 17, a Spurs win would bring the League title to North London. Wednesday had clung tenaciously to Spurs heels in a run of 19 League games without defeat; they had not lost since December 3. The kick-off on the Monday evening was put back to 8.00 to give the 62,000 capacity crowd more time to assemble. It was an atmosphere particulary suited to the swashbuckling Mackay as he sought to obliterate Bobby Craig, Wednesday's Scottish midfield driving force, from the action. But after half an hour Megson silenced the crowd with an opening goal for the visitors. But any self-doubts at Tottenham had now disappeared and they won the game before half-time. Three minutes before the break, Dyson belied nature to flick on Baker's cross for Smith to equalise, and two minutes later Norman strode forward to deflect Blanchflower's free-kick to Allen, who volleyed Spurs to the League title.

Now the double became a realistic prospect but though Spurs had reached the Cup Final there were many who felt that there was a jinx on such a feat ever taking place. The draw had been kind to Nicholson's team in the early rounds. In the third, they had been paired with Charlton Athletic, a middle-of-the-table Second Division side, who even so managed to stretch a Spurs side which was out of sorts with itself. Charlton battled back into the match at 3–2 and Spurs, far from their best, had been relieved that the scoreline remained that way.

A freakish quirk of the draw brought Crew Alexandra to White Hart Lane in the fourth round for the second successive year. In 1960 Tottenham had been held to a 2–2 draw at Gresty Road before exacting fearsome revenge in London by 13 goals to 2; Smith and Allen had shared ten of the haul between them. Now, fortified by a third round win over Chelsea at Stamford Bridge, Crewe gave an improved performance but only some phenomenal goalkeeping by Williamson prevented the 5–1 winning margin from stretching.

The fifth round took Spurs to Villa Park, an unlucky ground for them, particularly in the Cup where they had lost semi-finals to late goals in 1948, 1953, and 1956. But now another quirk of the fixtures took them to play Aston Villa in a League game a week before the Cup tie. In the midst of their indifferent spell, they still won 2–1, and the confidence exuded from them the following week when they scored twice in the first half. White, whose tragic death when struck by lightning was to so deprive Spurs three years later, created both scores in a personal display of great finesse.

An awkward trip to Sunderland followed in the sixth round, and in the cauldron of Roker Park Nicholson must have been happy to earn a replay. Another capacity crowd battled its way down the Tottenham High Road for the replay and they were not to be disappointed. Spurs struck their best form since the turn of the year, led by goals from Allen, Smith and Dyson by half-time, and won at a canter, 5–0.

The semi-final was played the week after the 3–2 League defeat at Cardiff, and it meant a return to Villa Park to meet Burnley; and with Sheffield United meeting Leicester City in the less distinguished semi-final, all were agreed that the winners at Villa Park would win the Cup. Well though Spurs played in the semi-final they were indebted for their survival to a series of acrobatic saves from Bill Brown to repel a Burnley attack which had drawn belief from the four goals they managed in the League game at White Hart Lane.

But just after the half hour Allen made a goal for Smith, and early in the second half the centre forward volleyed in a clearance for his second goal; the Spurs fans were already yelling 'When the Spurs Go Marching In' by the time White and Dyson broke clear in the last minute to make a third for Jones.

After two replays, Leicester finally overcame Sheffield United, but though they had won at Tottenham and finished sixth in the League, they had obtained 21 fewer points. That was a fair indication of the gap in class. Only the jinx of the 'double', it seemed, could stop Spurs winning at Wembley.

But it was another jinx – that peculiar to Wembley of depriving one side of a player with a serious injury – which exerted its fluence. And it worked against Leicester. After 18 minutes their right-back Chalmers twisted his knee in a clash with Allen and was forced to adopt a walking-on part on the right wing. Leicester responded magnificently to the hardship and Spurs were not the first side in history to discover the difficulty in breaking down the resolve of a side with ten fit men.

Allen and Dyson missed good opportunities, Jones had a goal disallowed for offside, and more than an hour had been played before the final step to history was taken. In the 66th minute, Allen, wide on the right touchline, turned a pass infield to Dyson; the tiny winger helped the ball on to Smith who received the ball with his back to the goal. But this muscular forward belied his rugged appearance with a deft touch and he twisted easily into a shooting position and hammered his shot past Banks at the near post. The double was won in that moment, though ten minutes later Smith's deep cross arrived at the far post, where a fit Chalmers would have cleared easily; instead, the unmarked Dyson flung himself forward to score, reward for a long season of unremitting endeavour.

Blanchflower, now 35 and recently elected Footballer of the Year for the second time, collected the FA Cup just as he had lifted the League trophy the previous week. Nicholson, a man given to reflective rather than immediate praise, had built an unforgettable team in just his second full season as manager, though his 25th at Tottenham. Nethertheless, so sparing was he with his laudatory remarks that Danny Blanchflower commented at the time, 'We've had what our manager might call a rather good year.'

That 'rather good year' choked the record books. In the League, Spurs' total of 66 points equalled Arsenal's record set up 30 years earlier; their 33 points from away matches was also equal to Arsenal's achievement in that same 1930–31 season. The opening run of 11 successive wins was also a new record, beating Hull City's nine in 1948. They won 31 League games, a new best in First Division history. They won 16 away games, which had never been previously accomplished. They had beaten 11 clubs home and away, a feat only twice managed before. They had reached 50 points in their 29th game, faster than any other club. And their 115 League goals was a club record. All this had been achieved by just 17 players – yet another record.

But above all, they had done the 'impossible'; they had won the double under 20th century conditions. And they had won it in a scintillant style. Blanchflower and his men had walked on the water.

STARS IN THE STADIUM OF LIGHT

*How Manchester United went to Lisbon and destroyed
Benfica*

Throughout the 1960s, Manchester United were fired with
one ambition. For all their commitment to the pursuit of
domestic honours, the team played with a burning desire to
win the European Cup. To all at Old Trafford there would be
no proper epitaph to the lives of the players and officials lost
in the tragedy of the Munich air crash until the trophy for
which those players were competing on that fateful trip rested
in their own cabinet.

In 1968 their thirst was finally quenched when they became
the first English club to win that competition. But even if they
had fallen short of that accolade they could have paid no
finer tribute to their lost colleagues than the performance they
gave in Lisbon in 1966, the most devasting 90 minutes ever
played by a British club in European competition.

Their opponents were Benfica, the pride of Portugal, and
at that time arguably the biggest power in Europe. As befitted
their nickname, the Eagles, they were in the 1960s the most
celebrated birds of prey in European competition, having won
the European Cup in 1961 and 1962 and being beaten finalists
in 1963 and 1965. The dusky Eusebio had blossomed into the
most dangerous striker in the continent, and within months
was to outscore the best in the world in England's World Cup.
Team-mates like the midfield provider Coluna, the elegant
forward Jose Augusto, the colossal striker Jose Torres and the
persistent winger Simoes were to be forces in the Pyrtugal

team which failed so gloriously to beat England and who finished, much praised, in third place.

And on March 9 1966 Benfica and their fanatical support in Lisbon awaited Manchester United, backed by the assurance of a narrow 3–2 defeat at Old Trafford in the first leg of their quarter-final. True, it had been a reward industriously gained. The pulsating atmosphere engendered, particularly at the baying Stretford End, had at times unsettled the Portuguese champions, and in a desperate opening David Herd had headed against a post. But Benfica had given early example of their class with a deliberately taken goal from Jose Augusto following Eusebio's corner.

The middle of the game belonged to United. The 19-year-old George Best, never perhaps properly credited for his superb passing ability, created an equaliser for Herd. Denis Law, with his enormous appetite for goals, fired in a second after Bobby Charlton had thrust the ball into his path. Then, with an hour played, Bill Foulkes, the centre-half who had survived Munich, pushed forward on the award of a free-kick, met Cantwell's accurate cross and headed a third.

A two-goal lead would have sent United to Lisbon in optimistic heart, but it was the Benfica players who were beaming at the final whistle, for minutes earlier Eusebio had manufactured their second goal. After peppering Gregg's goal with shots from all angles and ranges, he perhaps surprised the United defenders when he opted for the pass; they ignored the beanpole frame of Torres, who had time to turn in what appeared to be the crucial score. A win, then, for United but the moral success belonged to Benfica.

There was, after all, plenty of substance to the Benfica smirks that night in Manchester. Their home record in the European Cup was more than impressive – 18 wins in 19 ties in Lisbon, 78 goals from Eusebio and company at a cost of only 13 at their own end. As further proof of their potency, they had scored three or more goals on all but three of those 19 occasions, and the noise produced in their Stadium of Light by a capacity 80,000 crowd was even more oppressive to visiting teams than that at Old Trafford. Despite the 11 internationals in their line-up, the test that United faced was immense.

On March 9, Lisbon was gripped by the prospect of the confrontation between their own heroes and the champions of England. Fans flocked to the Stadium, many knowing that the journey was hopeless and that they would never see the game. Cars and coaches blocked the surrounding routes almost to the detriment of the night – referee Concetto Lo Bello from Italy only just reached the ground in time. The atmosphere inside gripped the pit of the stomach.

No extra spur was needed to ignite the mood of the followers of the Eagles, but the Benfica officials fanned the flames by arranging a presentation to Eusebio minutes before the kick-off. The near-pandemonium that followed delayed the start. As the fans roared, the dark-shirted United players had to battle with their inevitable nerves through an extended kick-in, looking almost extras to the star cast of Benfica players in their gleaming all-white strip.

Minutes earlier Matt Busby, perhaps the most fervent pursuer of United's European dream, had given his final dressing-room words of advice. He anticipated that the frenzied crowd would immediately drive Benfica on to the offensive. United's hopes would depend on how well they could rebuff the opening volleys. Busby urged his side to play it tight in the early stages – a policy of containment and organised defensive play in which the forwards would drop back to forge another link in the chain of resistance. Busby felt that the first quarter of an hour could decide his team's fate, but he could not have realised the absolute validity of his words. And when Pat Crerand smashed a mirror knocking a ball about the dressing-room, the omens did not look to be on United's side.

The youthful Best had received his share of criticism – his long hair and unconventional appearance had offended the more reactionary football followers – but no one had ever criticised his hearing. Yet his approach to the opening of the match suggested that his ears had missed all the wise counsel of his manager. Every time his deft touch brought the ball

109

under his control, he threatened the Benfica defence with his attacking runs. But above all, inside the first 12 minutes he outlined his definition of a policy of containment by scoring two goals.

The first after only half that time began when Charlton had been forced to the ground. The roaring Benfica afficionados barely gulped for breath as Tony Dunne approached the free-kick, sure in their minds that it was but the most minor mishap in the inevitable march towards glorious victory.

There was less excuse for a similar attitude taken by the Benfica defenders, for as Dunne struck the free-kick the goalmouth did not abound with urgency. Best capitalised on this moment of aberration to score excitingly with a spirited jump and excellently fashioned header. Like his passing skill, Best's power in the air is unfortunately unlikely to be remembered, but recall of it merely heightens the sadness at the terrible waste of his premature departure from football less than eight years from this memorable night.

When the ball hit the net, silence. As the masses slowly recovered from the shock Best raised his goalscoring hammer to stun them again. There seemed little danger to Costa Pereira's goal when the ball was in the arms of Gregg at the other end of the pitch. But David Herd outjumped centre-half Germano to nudge the goalkeeper's clearance into the path of Best. Manchester and English football already knew the capabilities of the lean, handsome Irishman, but now he was about to unveil his party-piece to an unsuspecting European audience.

The white-shirted defenders might as well have been ghosts for all the effect they had on Best's solo run. A drop of the shoulder, a sway of the hips and the acceleration of a sports car in overdrive left a trail of devastation until Costa Pereira became the last victim. Confronting the goalkeeper, Best retained his composure and placed his scoring shot into the corner of the net before turning into the embracing arms of his team-mates, the only people in the ground who could believe what they had just witnessed.

On aggregate, United now led by three goals and Benfica

were perhaps the only team in the world with the attacking strength to close that sort of gap. But within three minutes the question had become hypothetical as, incredibly, United scored again. Understandably buoyant, the United side, which contained several players with a flair for the theatrical, realised that they stood on a stage perfect for unveiling the extent of their repertoire of skills. Bobby Charlton, John Connelly, and Denis Law interpassed their way past a number of bemused opponents as though they were illustrating a point to youngsters on a training ground. Costa Periera, thoroughly exposed, had no chance as the interplay moved towards goal and the final pass left Connelly, the England winger, with a simple chance which he took with confidence. That opening period of 'anxiety' had passed and, more in obedience of their attacking instincts than at the call of their manager, Manchester United, in this graveyard of the hopes of so many European teams, led by three goals to nil; six-two on aggregate.

As Busby's team understandably paused for breath, the Eagles raised their heads and made a brave attempt to scale the mountain. But they found defenders as well equipped in destruction as their attackers had been in construction. The willing Foulkes competed bravely with the size of Torres and physically began to wear him down; Brennan and Dunne were sure on the flanks, and in the thick of the fray Stiles, bawling and encouraging with a velocity that penetrated even the most optimistic cries from the stands, sealed any holes. His tenacity also blunted the rapier of Eusebio's attack, the athletic forward from Mozambique becoming totally frustrated by the attentions of the unlikely looking toothless figure who was to be the symbol of England's World Cup win four months later. Stiles won a psychological victory that night in Lisbon that was to serve him well when the two players met in the colours of England and Portugal with a place in a World Cup final at stake.

But strangely, it was a moment of defensive chaos which cost United a quarter of their aggregate lead. Brennan showed a rare sign of tension when he disobeyed all the principles of back-passing by not taking note of Gregg's movements and by sending his pass in the direction of the goal. Gregg had advanced and was comprehensively beaten when the ball lobbed off the right-back's boot and looped in just under the cross-bar. But the slip did not breed any further panic and United's ship eased away from the proximity of rocks and resumed a stable course.

The eager Best was by now causing gasps of anxiety every time he got the ball, though he would be the first to admit that his fluency owed much to those around him. Herd, the unselfish foil, ran tirelessly, pulling the confused defenders this way and that as they sought to keep track of him. In any other team, Denis Law's menace would have earned him the attentions of at least two defenders, but Benfica had no men to spare, and the Scottish international was conspicuous in a team of stars and not just because of his flaxen hair. Pat Crerand, whose speed of thought more than compensated for a physical lack of pace, provoked the defence like a Chinese torturer, driving passes like darts at Benfica's weak areas. All this, plus Bobby Charlton at his best.

A three-one win for United would have been a sensational achievement. But with every player at the peak of his game, they created a new dimension in the final minutes of the tie. Crerand had made a career out of his harmony with Law, prising open the most unyielding of defences for his fellow Scot to capitalise on the chance with his deadly instincts. But now the roles were reversed and as Crerand stretched his legs into a forward run, Law's controlled pass gave him the ball; Denis could not have bettered Crerand's deliberate and accurate finish.

And still it was not over. Sensing the total bewilderment and frustration of the opposition, Bobby Charlton picked the ball up in the Benfica half and glided past one defender, slipped a second and dummied a third. By now even Costa Pereira's efforts had become no more than a token as Charlton added a majestic final touch. Benfica 1 Manchester United 5 – sports editors around the world were to query such a scoreline as a misprint when it was flashed at the final whistle.

After such scintillation, United immediately became favourites to win the trophy, but somehow the adrenalin inspired by that noisy night in Lisbon did not flow when in the first leg of the semi-final United visited Belgrade to take on the Partizan club. Admittedly a gamble of playing George Best did not pay off; Best had twisted a knee in England and his limping performance in Yugoslavia was to be his last game of the season. When he returned to Manchester he went straight into hospital for the removal of a cartilage.

Crammed full of confidence, United dominated the opening of the game in Belgrade, engineering enough chances to set up another scoreline of sensational proportions. But this time the marksmanship of Lisbon had given way to total inaccuracy, and the nearest they came to taking the lead was when Law shot against the bar. Handicapped by Best's injury, United lost their grip and Partizan established a two-goal lead to take to Old Trafford.

There, the elusiveness of Best against a packed defence was sorely missed. United surprisingly lacked sufficient subtlety and at times the teamwork to unsettle the organised Yugoslavs who resisted unwaveringly for an hour and a quarter. Then Stiles aimed yet another cross into a crowded goalmouth and Soskic, the Partizan keeper, who had begun to wear an invincible look, could only help the ball over the line. United had 15 minutes to take the tie to a third match, but even half-chances were hard to come by. Again the European dream had fallen short of reality.

Benfica were even more devastated by their thrashing. Their domestic form fled like air from a pricked balloon. Sporting Lisbon beat them to the Portuguese title, and after six successive sorties into the battles of the European Cup they forfeited their right to a place the following season. Just how poor their form became was emphasised by their elimination from the Portuguese Cup by Beira Mar, a side nowhere near Benfica's class.

For the rest of that season the fans of Lisbon were haunted by the memories of United's visit and their breathtaking display. But for all their painful recollections, the Portuguese supporters took one United player to their hearts. George Best had the swarthy good looks of a Latin, and his appeal in the

Stadium of Light had touched even the most bigoted Benfica fans. His long black hair earned him the title of 'El Beatle' and his image was beginning to outstrip even the most heralded pop stars.

As referee Lo Bello's final blast on the whistle ended United's night of triumph, Best might have feared a savage reception as the terraces emptied on to the field of play. One fan sprinted towards the young Irishman brandishing a dagger, but the motive was peaceable enough – a quest for a lock of Best's flowing mane. The story goes that another enchanted supporter presented the United forward with a caged bird which he gratefully accepted and intended to bring back to his Manchester lodgings. Unfortunately the immigration authorities did not take a similar philanthropic view and on the grounds of quarantine the bird remained in Portugal.

They did well to remember Best, for two years later an odd coincidence paired Benfica and Manchester United once again in the European Cup – but this time with the large silver Cup as the prize for the winner. The events in the Stadium of Light sent United into the game with tremendous confidence, and they had the extra advantage of reaching the final in the year it was to be staged at Wembley Stadium.

But Benfica resisted with resolution throughout the first 90 minutes. No goals to either side in the first half, and though a rare header from Bobby Charlton gave United the lead, Graca restored the equilibrium with a goal nine minutes from full-time. But in extra time Best turned the tie with a goal which brought more than a passing memory of his individual effrontery in the Stadium of Light. Now his supporting cast had changed – it was Stepney not Gregg who effected the long clearance, and it was Kidd not Herd who made the aerial flick – but the brilliance of Best remained constant. He surged clear of Cruz, a defender he had tormented in Lisbon, made light of another attempted tackle, sold the most insolent of dummies on Henrique, Costa Pereira's successor, and rolled the ball into the empty net. Kidd and Charlton added further goals to inflate that scoreline, but in that moment of magic

Best had sealed another victory over Benfica. He, above all, had shown the power to clip the wings of the Eagles.

This time there was gold at the end of the rainbow. Matt Busby had achieved his greatest ambition, and the European Cup would be on show in the Old Trafford boardroom. It had been a long struggle that had taken Busby and his team many thousands of miles across Europe, and since 1958 every trip must have brought aching memories of that fateful February day in Munich.

And if the Benfica fans quibbled about losing the final on what was a far from neutral ground, they had only to cast their minds back to the events of two years earlier. Though United shone at Wembley, their most dazzling performance found the perfect setting in the Stadium of Light.

A PROPHECY FULFILLED

The story of the World Cup final, 1966

At 5.15 on the afternoon of Saturday July 30 1966, one of the most ambitious of footballing prophesies became dramatically fulfilled. Since his installation as England's team manager more than three years earlier, Alf Ramsey had insisted with uncharacteristic candour that England would win the 1966 World Cup. But even he could not have anticipated the almost fictional fluctuations of a final which saw his team virtually have to win the Jules Rimet trophy twice!

If the England team began the tournament as favourites to win their first World Cup, it was surely because they held home advantage – all their matches were to be staged in the familiar setting of Wembley Stadium. The welcome introduction of Ramsey's professional ideas and practices to what had been a sector of football run by amateurs had improved the consistency of England's results, but he approached the 1966 World Cup without a completely settled team.

In a series of warm-up games including a tour of Scandinavia and Poland, names like Tambling, Eastham, Callaghan, Gerry Byrne, Connelly, Hunter, and Paine were given their chance to establish themselves before England met Uruguay to open the World Cup finals, and a young West Ham forward called Geoff Hurst appeared to have forfeited his chance with a fumbling performance on a bumpy pitch in Copenhagen.

But the defence had fallen into place. Gordon Banks, under pressure from Bonetti and the veteran Ron Springett, had been stimulated to clinch the goalkeeper's spot. George Cohen, the willing Fulham full-back, was a fitness fanatic, and thus able to surge forward into attacking positions, using the vacant spaces along the touchlines in Ramsey's 'wingless' formation. The more elegant Ray Wilson was perhaps the most complete full-back in the tournament.

Jack Charlton's Bobby's elder brother, but a late developer at centre-half, had proven his international quality over the previous 12 months, but the key defensive spot belonged to Bobby Moore, the captain and the purveyor of Ramsey's philosophies on the field. Initially, it had been an uneasy liaison between manager and skipper, but after Moore had been disciplined on an American tour two years earlier, an unyielding bond of respect had been forged.

In Spain in December 1965, Ramsey had dabbled with a formation of four defenders, three midfield players, and three attackers. The experiment had prospered on that night with a convincing win over fellow qualifiers for the finals. The charismatic Nobby Stiles, short of stature and of sight, but a belligerent acquirer of the ball, and Bobby Charlton, converted from an enigmatic forward, who could use the possession that Stiles would win, were two who had established midfield places.

Liverpool's Roger Hunt and the prolific Jimmy Greaves of Tottenham Hotspur were two guaranteed of their places in attack. Hunt, whose discipline to his team's needs often obscured his own talents, was cast in Ramsey's methodical mould. Greaves, more the individual, was just the opposite, but his goals seemed to be a vital factor were England to succeed.

The other two places were undecided even as England began their Group matches. Against Uruguay the precocious Alan Ball held a midfield place, while Ramsey, still not abandoning his quest for the right type of winger – one who would graft as well as attack along the touchline – plumped for John Connelly. The result – a goalless draw – merely emphasised that the blend was not yet satisfactory.

For the second Group game, versus Mexico, Ball's place went to the gangling Martin Peters, a versatile youngster from West Ham who epitomised his club side's philosophy of pure football; it was only his fourth full cap. Terry Paine, another winger, replaced Connelly. England, with goals from Bobby Charlton and Hunt, won 2–0.

Peters remained, but Paine became the next discard for the final qualifying tie against France. Liverpool's Ian Callaghan became the third in Ramsey's elusive search for the right man to attack down the touchline. Another 2–0 win was the outcome, with two goals from Hunt, but the feeling of uneasiness still prevailed. Despite Ramsey's much-publicised promise, England did not look World Champions, as they joined West Germany, Argentina, Russia, Portugal, gallant North Korea, Uruguay, and Hungary in the quarter-finals.

It was for the quarter-final against Argentina, that the jigsaw finally fell into place. Ramsey made two more changes, one by necessity. Greaves, goalless in the three games, injured a leg against France and was out; Geoff Hurst, who had felt that his performance in Denmark had ruled him out of the reckoning, was his replacement. Ramsey, despairing of his orthodox wingers, turned again to Alan Ball. Hunt and Hurst were to be the striking force; Ball and Peters became midfield players with extra responsibilities to get into scoring positions.

Hurst's match-winning header from Peters' cross ensured a semi-final place. Nor could the rowdiness of the Argentinians, which culminated in the sending-off of Rattin, obscure the excellence of England's performance. Three days later the same side disposed of Portugal in perhaps the classic individual game of the whole tournament, and at last Ramsey's prophesy looked to be more than a forlorn boast.

Eusebio's late penalty for Portugal had been the first goal conceded by England's organised defence. Hurst's power in the penalty area had added a new dimension to the attack. Though he had not scored against Portugal, his strength in holding off defenders had directly engineered one of the two goals scored by Bobby Charlton. And on the smooth surface of Wembley his suspect control was not letting him down.

From the other half of the draw, the emergence of West Germany into the final added nationalistic overtones to what was to be a titanic struggle. The pressure on the players to win was already enormous; it became further magnified by the memories of a large portion of the country who could recall relatively recent conflict between the two countries in a less sporting event.

The Germans, managed by Helmut Schoen, who had been the assistant to Sepp Herberger during their World Cup triumph of 1954, had topped Group Two to qualify for the later stages of the competition. They had scored four goals without reply to eliminate Uruguay in the quarter-finals, before beating Russia 2–1 to reach the Wembley final.

But in many ways it had been a strange and controversial pattern of progress. There were talented individuals in the side, none more so than Franz Beckenbauer, on the threshold of an outstanding career as one of the great post-War internationals. Used in midfield, his grace and awareness had brought him four goals in the qualifying games and created several others. Schulz and Schnellinger were defenders of the highest class. Overath, much admired by Ramsey, added industry as well as skill to the midfield. Held and Emmerich provided pace and strength to an attack in which the most potent goalscorer was the blond, stocky Helmut Haller.

But controversy surrounded West Germany. Albrecht of Argentina, Troche and Silva of Uruguay, and Chislenko of Russia, were all sent off playing against them. The Germans had a tendency to over-react when fouled. The two sets of facts were not unrelated. They also became over-defensive at the slightest threat of danger, as if not completely believing in the abundance of their own talent. Beckenbauer, such an asset going forward, would be withdrawn into deep defence or blunted by orders to perform a negative marking job.

The atmosphere on the day of the final gave the lie to the belief that the British are a conservative race who do not air their emotion in public. The route of the England coach from the team headquarters in Hendon to the Stadium was flooded with cheering well-wishers; streets and shops were festooned with banners and Union Jacks; the occasion transcended the boundary of mere football support. The whole country became emotionally enmeshed in the fortunes of England's footballers; indeed the eventual success was to provide a boost to attendances throughout the following domestic season.

England had no injury worries. Greaves, arguably the greatest of England's goalscorers, was fit again, and some critics lobbied for his return. Ramsey plumped for Hurst, and announced the side that had defeated Argentina. West Germany had toyed with the idea of making a change in goal, but the young reserve, Maier, was not fit, so Tilkowski retained his place.

There was plenty in the past record of meetings between the two countries to give England confidence; of nine previous internationals England had won eight and the other had been drawn; the two teams had met twice in the previous 14 months, England triumphing in Nuremburg and at Wembley by solitary goal margins. But England and West Germany had never met in such a cauldron of atmosphere before.

The England players felt optimistic. Bobby Charlton recalls that he watched the West Germany semi-final against Russia and that the players were relieved that the Germans and not the Russians had won. Ramsey, an overt optimist in this particular cause for over three years, also had no doubts that England would win.

But the events of the first quarter of an hour would soon unsettle the firmest beliefs in an England success. After the preliminary tentative jousts set against a cacophony of sound, it was West Germany who made the first real incision. Tilkowski had needed treatment after a collision with Hurst, and then turned aside a long range drive from Peters before Uwe Seeler, now a World Cup veteran, found some space on the left.

The ball pulled in with the right foot gave the advantage to the defender rather than the attackers, but one slip surrendered that advantage. Ray Wilson, faultless throughout the competition, moved forward to meet the ball; no German jumped with him. A defender of such finesse that a straightforward clearance header was not for him, he aimed to nod the ball down for a better-placed colleague to start a counter-attack. But his aim went awry.

The ball dropped free inside the England penalty area, straight into the path of Helmut Haller. The German had not squandered such chances in the previous games in the competition, and he did not miss now, pulling his shot across and beyond Gordon Banks with his right foot and into the far corner. Thirteen minutes of the World Cup Final had passed, and England were a goal behind. England had scored only seven goals in their five previous games; now at least two were needed to realise Ramsey's prophesy.

Surprisingly, only six minutes elapsed before an equaliser was fashioned, and its making was a tribute to the vision of England's captain. Carrying the ball into the German half, Moore was caught and tripped by Overath. The use of the free-kick was deadly. As Charlton called for a short ball to the left touchline. Moore and Hurst recognised a situation from which they had profited at club level for West Ham. Hurst had begun his run from the far post before the free-kick had been taken. As it curved in he had already left his marker useless behind, and as he and the ball arrived at the near post he was totally unmarked. By then the finish remained relatively simple – a straightforward though totally decisive header – but it had been a goal created as much from within the head as without.

The initiative swung to the home side. Though Peters was in trouble for some shirt-tugging, England's rhythm was established. Hunt thrust all his power behind a shot which Tilkowski saved with difficulty before the Germans recovered some composure. Banks was forced into a double save first from Overath and then as the ball rolled free from Emmerich; Seeler, too, manufactured a looping drive, which the England goalkeeper twisted to turn over the bar.

For supporters of both sides, the unpredictability of the match was matched by the vagarities of the weather; sunshine and showers on the pitch and above it. The second half began in the middle of a shower and the flamboyance of both sides seemed dampened. The cautious side of the German plan had again involved the withdrawal of Beckenbauer to devote his attentions to the stifling of Bobby Charlton. It provided an intriguing battle for the purists amongst the audience, but for the majority of the crowd it was simply two enormously gifted players cancelling out each other's threat. But even Beckenbauer was powerless when an astute deflection from Hurst's temple set up a shooting chance. But Charlton's effort fell beyond Tilkowski's far post.

Appropriately it was the willing Hurst who played a part in the move which broke an ever tightening deadlock with less than a quarter of an hour remaining. Ball, whose energy had not been sapped by the tension or by his own prodigious efforts, busied himself on the right and won a corner. The kick was an orthodox outswinger, but caused sufficient confusion to allow Hurst to turn on the edge of the area and try an optimistic shot. It was blocked, but carried sufficient velocity to balloon upwards and on into the goal area. Amazingly it dropped in front of an unmarked Martin Peters, barely six yards from the line. A youngster could have been forgiven for snatching at and wasting the opportunity, but Peters' technique and composure matched the occasion and England were ahead.

That should have been that. The England players whose concessions throughout the tournament had been but a penalty and Haller's goal felt sure that they had won. That the victory was not clinched then and that Martin Peters will not be remembered as the man who scored the winner in a World Cup final hung on a contentious decision from referee Gustav Dienst of Switzerland. With the game in its last breaths, Jack Charlton was adjudged to have pushed Held as he headed clear. Dienst gave West Germany the free-kick 25 yards from Banks' goal.

Emmerich, a disappointing, impotent force throughout the match, took the kick with his powerful left foot and drove it despairingly into England's defensive wall. The inevitable deflection fell for West Germany. Via Held, the ball bobbled across the face of the goal. It appeared to brush Schnellinger's hand before dropping invitingly in front of Weber, the centre-back. From such short range Banks had no chance. From the very precipice of defeat West Germany had clawed a path back and were very much alive. England had just time to kick-off before extra time was signalled.

As the Germans celebrated, Ramsey's team sank to the turf disbelievingly. Jack Charlton sat, his head in his hands. Others stood, their mouths still open from the shock. Only the arrival on the pitch of the England manager restored the sense of purpose; Ramsey, showing no emotion, offered a simple message, 'You've won it once. Now go out and win it again.' Character would now be as critical as skill.

The 93,000 crowd did not have to wait long to discover whether England possessed strength of purpose as well as strength of limb in their reserves. Alan Ball symbolised the attitude. In the opening minutes of extra time, he tore past Schnellinger as though he was a fresh recruit to the conflict, and his fulminating shot nearly beat Tilkowski. That must have frightened the Germans, who surely believed that they had won the psychological battle. More alarm, too, when Charlton was on target from the edge of the penalty area and Tilkowski needed the post as an ally to keep the ball out.

Ten minutes into extra time, England regained their lead – Ball again the inspiration, Schnellinger again a spectator. The little red-head from Blackpool turned in a cross from the right and found Hurst. The ball did not come easily to the big forward, but with his back half to the goal his control did not fail him. One touch took the pace from Ball's pass and as he pivoted he swept the ball above Tilkowski and against the underside of the crossbar. Then down and then out, to be cleared by Weber.

Hunt, the nearest English forward, stood arms aloft, apparently certain the ball had crossed the line. The agitated German defenders took the opposite view. The referee appeared undecided. But one man, the Russian linesman, Bakhramov, was sure. 'Yes,' he signalled, the ball had bounced down behind the line. The goal stood. The relief boomed out from the crowd.

If England had Ball, West Germany had their physical inspiration in the dedicated running of Held and Overath, and while other players dragged the last reserves from their aching limbs these two pulled their side back into the game as it moved into the second period of extra time. Held, apparently inexhaustible, twice ripped holes in the England defence without achieving the final penetration. For the rest Moore remained steadfast, propping up his suffering colleagues, particularly Wilson, who was groggy from a bang on the skull. Could there be another dramatic equaliser?

Moore himself provided the answer. Always aware that an aimless clearance would simply refurnish the opposition with possession, he had the presence of mind and the strength of body to play a last minute clearance from his own lines up to Geoff Hurst. Hurst, too, remained mentally alert, and his one thought was to carry the ball as far away from his own goal as he could possibly manage. It was only when he had crossed the half way line that he realised that he had left West Germany behind, and that his run had taken him in at Tilkowski's goal.

As his weakening legs began to protest, his final thought was to hit the ball as hard as possible so that even if it flew high and wide precious seconds would be used up returning it to play. But the shot was unerring; left-footed it flashed high to Tilkowski's right. Hurst had a hat-trick. England had won the World Cup, but incredibly Ramsey, forever the analyst, recalls that he was admiring Overath, for being the only German to chase Hurst's run, as the ball rocketed into the netting.

Certainly the triumph belonged to Hurst, the goalscoring hero, to Moore, the calculating captain, voted the tournament's best player, to Bobby Charlton and Banks, world class performers and to the remainder of the players. But above all it belonged to Alf Ramsey, the man who had lived up to his boast. Within a relatively short span he had instilled method, organisation, and flair into an ailing international set-up. As a player he had been present at the downfall in 1953 at the hands of Hungary. Now he had settled the score with the proudest win in the whole history of England's international life.

When the ballyhoo had passed, cynics suggested that England had won because they were at home, and that in the final they had had the advantage of an arguable third goal, that the overall standard from the competing countries had been low. But Ramsey had cut his cloth according to the demands of the situation. In an era of functional football, he had created a side designed to outfunction its opponents. It would be utterly churlish to all he achieved to deny what England achieved on that showery Saturday in July. For in 1966 England were the best in the world!

'JOCK, YOU'RE IMMORTAL NOW!'

How Celtic became the first British winners of the European Cup

There can be few more unlikely scenes pertaining to a European Cup triumph than that which took place in the manager's office on the ground of the Welsh League side Llanelli in 1951.

A 28-year-old half-back called Jock Stein had arrived to tell his manager that he was leaving the club and retiring; a couple of burglaries at the house he had kept on back in Scotland had reinforced his decision, but the real reason was his feeling that after an unproductive spell with Albion Rovers and a year with Llanelli he could go no further in the game.

But the manager, unaware of Stein's problems, had news of his own to impart. Of all clubs, Celtic had made an inquiry about signing Stein, aiming to ulitise his experience to bring on the youngsters in their second eleven. It was the beginning of an outstanding relationship between man and club which, as a player and then as manager, brought an unending number of trophies to Parkhead. And 16 years after that confrontation in Llanelli came the greatest triumph of all; in the 12th year of the competition, Celtic at last wrote the name of a British winner on the elusive European Cup.

The charisma of Stein was immediately in evidence when he arrived at Celtic as a player. Injuries forced a temporary abandonment of the club's plans to use him in the reserve team, and Stein so revelled in the opportunity of first-team football that those plans were eventually dropped. His own solid game became more appreciated now that, for the first time in his career, he was playing alongside top-class performers. Celtic made him captain, and with Bobby Evans and the Irish left-half Bertie Peacock, Stein completed a half-back line of the highest calibre.

In the 1953–54 season, he completely overtook those painful days at Albion Rovers and Llanelli by leading Celtic to the Scottish League title and the Scottish Cup, their first double for 40 years, and he continued to lead by example until an ankle injury ended his playing days. Then, as coach, he nurtured and developed young talents like those of Pat Crerand, who was to blossom into one of the great creative wing-halves for Manchester United and Scotland, and Billy Mc-Neill, later his lieutenant in a glorious decade at Parkhead.

Stein cut his managerial teeth at Dunfermline, and in the direst of circumstances. When he was appointed early in 1960, Dunfermline seemed certain to be relegated with only eight matches to play. But so instantaneous was the effect of Stein's powers of motivation and strategy that his new side won six games in succession and saved themselves. The next year he completed a phenomenal revitalisation by leading them to a Scottish Cup victory, their first major honour.

His job done, he moved on to Hibernian and, though he spent under a year at Easter Road, won the Summer Cup, and Hibs were competing for the League title when he left. They separated when the offer came to rejoin Celtic as manager – an appointment which flew in the face of tradition at the Catholic club, for Jock Stein is a Protestant. There can be no greater indication than that of the value that the Celtic directors placed on his services!

When he returned to Parkhead in 1965, no one knew better than Stein that Celtic had not won the Scottish League since his own day in 1954. Surely not even he could have foreseen that they were to take the title for the next nine seasons! But not only did he create a successful side in Scotland. Within a short time Jock Stein's Celtic was to earn the deserved respect of the world.

Within a month of Stein's return Celtic won the Scottish Cup to earn a place in Europe for the 1965–66 season, and it was this experience which paved the way for their most fulfilling moment the following year when, after winning the League title, they qualified for the European Cup.

Stein has always been a players' man, and his rapport with his professionals has always been a factor in his triumphs. In 1965 it was not his style to turn the staff upside down in the quest for success, but by a combination of quiet counsel, out and out bullying, and a physical fitness programme which would have made a Sergeant Major blanche, he breathed new life into his staff.

His goalkeeper, Ronnie Simpson, was in his mid-30s and had only lasted that long because he had come under the magic touch when Stein was with Hibernian. Simpson had made his name in two earlier decades; in 1944 he had played for Queen's Park as a 14-year-old, and four years later he played for Great Britain in the 1948 Olympics. After turning professional with Third Lanark, he tasted glory with Newcastle United and collected Cup-Winners' medals in 1952 and 1955 before being given away to Hibernian. There Stein had copied his own boss at Llanelli by selling an experienced player to bring on the reserves at Celtic, but when Stein returned to Parkhead he brought Simpson back into the spotlight and in 1967 – 23 years after his debut – 36-year-old Ronnie Simpson was to win his first Scottish cap.

Stein encouraged the tall Tommy Gemmell to ulitise his attacking flair from the left-back position, and Gemmell, too, developed into an all-purpose defender of international class. He converted the deceptively chunky Bobby Murdoch from an average performer at inside-forward to a perceptive goal-scoring wing-half – and again fashioned an international player. John Clark, a solid defender but never at his best in a creative role, was restricted to a job in the heart of the defence alongside Billy McNeill, and Stein's awareness of a player's limitations again reaped rich dividends, for Clark, too, was to wear the blue shirt of Scotland.

He did buy, to strengthen his attack, and wisely. Joe McBride had failed in English football but became Scotland's top goalscorer when brought from Motherwell for under £25,000, and when McBride had a serious injury Willie

Wallace achieved a consistency under Stein that he had never quite managed for Hearts.

But perhaps Stein's greatest managerial achievement came in his harnessing of the tempestuous Bertie Auld to Celtic's cause. Auld, a left-winger who could never exert the same mastery over himself that he could over the ball, had left Celtic for Birmingham City in 1961, where by his own standards he had flopped. Celtic brought him back in 1965 just before they recaptured Stein, but Stein saw Auld suited for a role in midfield, and such was his thoroughness that he organised a tour of America behind which the real purpose was to try out Auld in this role. Not only was Auld's form a revelation, but his mood responded to Stein's influence.

So it was on this basis, and with the encouragement of a run to the semi-final of the Cup-Winners' Cup in 1966, when they rather unluckily lost to Liverpool 2–1 on aggregate, that Celtic began their European Cup campaign the following season.

In an era of Italian successes based on a defensive outlook, Celtic's methods bordered on heresy. Stein gave every player his head; if Gemmell's surges into goalscoring positions caught the eye most, he was by no means the only defender to do so, and so fit had the players become under Stein's training methods that forwards covered for defenders and *vice versa* in fluent, ever-changing patterns.

At the time, the idealism of this philosophy looked foolish in the practical world of European football. Inter and AC Milan had won three of the last four European Cups with an approach at the other extreme, but Celtic came through their first round tie with impressive ease against Zurich, beating them on aggregate by five clear goals.

Nantes fell second round victims, beaten home and away 3–1, with forwards Steve Chalmers and Bobby Lennox scoring in both legs, and Celtic's first major problems did not arise until the quarter-finals. The champions of Yugoslavia, Vojvodina of Novisad, provided skilled and physically powerful opposition, and they won their home leg with a goal halfway through the second half. They missed chances to clinch the tie in the opening minutes at Parkhead. It was well into the second half when a goalkeeping error presented Chalmers with the goal that levelled the aggregate score, and then not until injury time did Celtic snatch their winner – a priceless header by McNeill from a corner.

Willie Wallace made his European debut in the semi-final in place of McBride, whose knee injury robbed Celtic of the services of their leading scorer for the second half of the season. Against Dukla Prague he began in style; after an hour's play at Parkhead it was 1–1, Johnstone having put Celtic ahead, then Wallace spun quickly to restore the lead and capitalised on a quickly taken free kick from Auld to increase it. In Czechoslovakia Celtic showed they could defend as well as attack and a goalless draw won them a place in the final against the masters of Italian chessboard football, Inter Milan.

Inter, as penny-pinching as ever in defence, had conceded just three goals in reaching the final, two of them to CSKA Sofia in the semi-final. They had beaten Moscow Torpedo, Vasas Budapest, and holders Real Madrid in the earlier rounds with hardly a hint of vulnerability, though they needed a play-off to beat the Bulgarians after two 1–1 draws. Their considerable experience of European finals and their total professionalism weighed the odds of beating Celtic heavily in their favour.

But Jock Stein ensured that Celtic would not lack self-belief, and his job was made easier by the retention of the League title and the 2–0 triumph over Aberdeen at Hampden Park to lift the Scottish Cup. But he was not going to sacrifice any principles to obtain a result – a pre-final screening of the 1960 European Cup final classic between Real Madrid and Eintracht Frankfurt indicated to his squad just what heights were expected of them.

Both sides had been robbed of key players by injuries. Celtic would miss the opportunism of McBride; Inter were certainly the weaker for the absence of their virtuoso inside-forward Luis Suarez and their ageing Brazilian winger Jair. But in Portugal's National Stadium on a sun-drenched evening in late May the mood of the neutrals was quite apparent – the flair of Celtic made them the more popular side, but rationale said that Inter must win.

The Italians could not have got off to a better start. Under manager Helenio Herrara their philosophy was undisguised – to obtain an early goal and then defend the advantage in an organised, calculated, and cynical manner. Sandro Mazzola might have scored in the first real attack had not Simpson kicked out to block the Italian international's well-placed header. But there was no escape after seven minutes when Mazzola and Corso worked the ball to Cappellini in a position where he could attack Jim Craig. The Celtic right-back, inside his own penalty area, mistimed his tackle and sent Cappellini and Scottish hopes tumbling to the ground.

There could be no disputing the penalty, nor Mazzola's keenness to take it. He had vowed to score on the ground which saw the last appearance of his famous father before he was killed in the plane crash at Superga which wiped out the entire Torino side in 1948. Simpson could not compete with such resolve, bought Mazzola's dummy, and Inter had obtained the early goal so necessary to their plans.

Now the Italians slotted easily into the 'catenaccio' system of defence, leaving at most one forward up the field. They willingly conceded possession to Celtic, fortified in the knowledge that even with the ball few teams could ruffle their discipline and composure. But they must have been surprised with the speed and variety of Celtic as the Scottish champions tore into the attack from all angles, their own swagger fortified by an increasing awareness that Inter appeared to have neither ambition nor aptitude for the counter-attack.

The pressure was incessant, but Inter resisted. As gaps opened Picci was the defender who usually acted instantly to block them. Celtic were allowed no time to adjust their sights as chances appeared and disappeared in a flash, and even when a shot was allowed to penetrate the blue and black striped shield of protection, Sarti in goal provided a magnificent last line of defence. And when all else failed the Italians had two moments of great fortune.

First Bertie Auld, playing the part of the returned prodigal with gusto, sensed a fleeting opening before him and set himself for a shot that smacked off the crossbar with a resonance which could be heard above the crowd's roar. Then Gemmell, now more in the front line than the rear, curled a centre which for once avoided Sarti's radar scanner of anticipation and also bounced off the woodwork to the advantage of Herrera's side.

When Sarti produced a miracle save from Auld, it looked as though Celtic were again to be another side of fine ideas to be undone by a slavish policy of defence – Sarti must have been unsighted as Auld blazed away through a mass of bodies, but the goalkeeper, diving backwards, downed the arms already upraised in triumph with a prodigious effort of reaction.

But Celtic showed no reaction to these reverses, and as the game moved deeper into the second half, desperation and over-elaboration were happily lacking from their play. And after an hour's play – almost to the second – reward came as though the fates had set a time-limit on Inter's good fortune.

Any type of scrambled goal would have suited Celtic's interest, but they contrived a score of perfect testimony to their style and ambition. One full-back, Craig, set off on a supporting run down the right touchline, sensed that defenders were positioning themselves for the orthodox high cross, and perceptively picked out the other full-back, Gemmell, who was sprinting forward towards the penalty area. He took the pass at the peak of his momentum and Sarti might as well have been asked to arrest the path of a meteorite for all the chance he had of preventing Gemmell's fulminating shot.

Inter now faced a problem. Their conditioning for League matches in Italy deemed that a draw would be a reasonable return should a lead be lost. But not in a European final. And as they struggled to alter course on to the offensive, Celtic still stormed forward. Sarti's reflexes continued to keep the game open, but the Inter forwards, for all their nimble work on the ball, had not the pace or the directness to embarass McNeill and his henchmen.

Apart from the occasional stuttering foray, Inter were now defending by necessity, no longer out of choice, but they resisted until just six minutes from time. Gemmell, in the centre of everything, again stimulated the attack, placing the ball into the path of Murdoch – a midfield player with the goalsense of an out and out forward. Throughout the game he had been always willing to take the responsibility of shooting from a distance, and again he set his bearings and drove at the Italian goal. Just how embarrassing the shot might have been for Sarti no one will ever know, because as the ball sped into the goal area, Chalmers quite deliberately stretched out his right foot and added a deflection. The result posed a problem to which even Sarti's amazing reactions could not find an answer. So Celtic, trailing almost from the off, now led well into the home straight.

The final six minutes lived long, not just for the Scottish patriots who unbridled their fervour by leaping the moat surrounding the ground to embrace the Celtic team at the final whistle, but also for all supporters of British football who had waited eleven years since the inception of the competition, for a British victory. To win would have been enough, but the verve and flamboyance of Celtic's victory added another dimension.

It came at a time when many successful sides had been preaching the wrong gospel, and with the match being screened live all over Europe, Celtic had provided the perfect answer to the rigorous drabness of Italian football. Even Helenio Herrera, the chief advocate of Italy's doctrines, was moved to say after the game that Celtic had deserved their win and that 'although we lost, the match was a victory for sport.' Certainly Celtic had offered a much more appealing alternative *modus operandi* to the millions of viewers watching the match on television.

For Jock Stein, in only his second full season in charge of the club, it was a vindication of all his attacking ideals. 'The best place to defend,' he had said so often, 'is in the other team's penalty area.' In Celtic's jubilant dressing-room, as he let the first feelings of victory wash over him, he was accosted by none other than Bill Shankly, who was reacting more like a Celtic fanatic than the manager of a rival club. 'Jock, you're immortal now!' was the cry from that familiar grating voice, and even allowing for some characteristic Shankly over-statement, there were a lot of Scots in Lisbon who would have thrown anyone into the moat around that Lisbon pitch if they had dared to deny that claim.

AWAY THE LADS!

The romance and the reality of Sunderland's FA Cup

When Sunderland of the Second Division overturned Arsenal in the semi-final of the 1973 FA Cup and against all the odds qualified to meet Leeds United at Wembley, the omens could not have escaped Don Revie. This man, who ran Leeds United with more belief in superstitions than any witches coven, must have nurtured a secret fear at the chronological conundrum which greeted the Roker Park side's appearance in the final. Their last Wembley visit had been in 1937 – a 3–1 victory over Preston North End – and a return in 1973 suggested that Fate would provide a result in Sunderland's favour.

It was at such straws that all but the most fanatical North-Easterner grasped, because logically there was no way that Sunderland could win. But for the arrival of Bob Stokoe as manager six months earlier, May might have been a time for lamenting a drop into the Third Division rather than lauding over a visit to Wembley. In that short space of time Stokoe had fashioned a remarkable improvement in League results, plus a Cup run that had, in Arsenal and Manchester City, accounted for two of the previous four Cup winners. Surely Leeds, the holders, would be different.

As had become the custom during Don Revie's reign at Elland Road, Leeds were in at the kill in all the major competitions. They finally finished third in the League after losing out in a dog-fight of a finish to Liverpool, the eventual winners, and Arsenal. Later in May they were to face AC Milan in the final of the European Cup-Winners' Cup. Most of Revie's squad were full internationals, completely inured to the pressures of a big occasion; many of Stokoe's squad had never visited Wembley Stadium even as spectators! Above all the total professionalism that characterised the Leeds mode of play would surely mean that they would in no way make the mistake of under-estimating their opponents.

To the logical mind, Sunderland were simply making up the numbers; just reaching the final being sufficient reward for the tremendous revival induced by that son of the North-East, Stokoe. It had been to this man, who was an integral part of the Newcastle United Cup successes of the early 1950s, that the Sunderland directors had turned in their hour of need. Around the time that Stokoe had been starring as a player on Tyneside, the club on the River Wear had earned the tag of the 'Bank of England side' as they paid out a succession of huge fees for the era to bring big names to Roker Park. It was a policy which proved yet again that success could not be bought.

But in November 1972 there was little money available to strengthen the side which was floundering in the bottom reaches of Division Two. What was in the coffers was passed on to Blackpool, not for a player, but as compensation to secure the release of Stokoe. On the surface it appeared the last throw of desperate gamblers, because Stokoe's managerial record with a succession of lower grade clubs, like Bury, Carlisle, Rochdale, and Charlton, had been little more than average. Hindsight shows that it was the move of the decade.

If he was lucky, it was in that he had talented players at Roker Park awaiting his arrival, but there was a desperate need for organisation and an injection of confidence. Dave Watson was a case in point. He had been an expensive buy from Rother-ham, a player cast in the mould of John Charles, able to use his leggy skills and heading ability to equal effect in defence or in attack. When Stokoe arrived at Roker Park Watsons' per-formance that season typified the club's problems. He had played 13 games at centre-forward without a goal to his name. But the new manager switched him back to centre-half, and as well as being the focal point of the defence he re-gained his scoring touch, coming forward to good effect at set-pieces.

Stokoe also restored confidence in Billy Hughes, a forward who at his best had the pace and inclination to attack defenders with the ball. Hughes had been in and out of favour at the start of the season, but Stokoe found the right blend for him and Dennis Tueart, a similar type of player, by buying Vic Halom, a burly, unselfish front runner who had scored his share of useful goals for Orient, Fulham, and Luton.

Another buy was full-back Ron Guthrie, from Stokoe's old club Newcastle, a reliable defender who helped seal up the left side of the rearguard. But for the rest it was a case of perming whoever was already on the staff; there was no money left for drastic refurbishing. Stokoe had the advantage of the gifted and consistent Jimmy Montgomery in goal, an experienced man who passed 400 League appearances during the season. Ian Porterfield, a Scot with the sort of creative left foot that managers dream about, was less consistent but had the ability to manufacture from midfield, as did the pint-sized Bobby Kerr, who had fought off the set-backs of two broken legs. Dick Malone, yet another import from over the border, was a somewhat ungainly right-back who nevertheless possessed enough flair to contribute when going forward.

Two youngsters completed the side – Richie Pitt, who had seen First Division action at a very tender age, held off the challenge of David Young to slot in alongside Watson at the back, while Micky Horswill, an ultra-competitive 19-year-old with red hair and a temper to match, earned a regular place as the ball-winning midfield man.

These players, under the astute guidance of Stokoe, had still been bent on the task of righting their League position when the FA Cup came round. Sunderland were 19th when they beat Notts County in the third round after a replay; Watson, from the back, scoring in both games against his first club. They had risen to 17th by the time Fourth Division Reading held them to a draw at Roker Park in the next round; but Sunderland won comfortably enough at Elm Park. But a 4–0 League win over Middlesbrough took them to Maine Road Manchester in something like the form that was to stun the country over the last two months of the season.

Opportunist goals from Horswill and Hughes earned yet another replay, and Roker Park was crammed full for the second game. Those who had returned for the first time for months must have marvelled in the change of attitude and aptitude of the same players who had been jeered at the start of the year. Hughes had a breath-taking 90 minutes, scoring twice; Halom added another scintillating goal. City, apart from a brief revival spurred by a Lee goal, were sunk. It was a contrast totally mirrored in the sixth round. Luton had won comfortably two-nil at Roker Park in October at a time when the decline had really set in; then, ironically, Halom had been one of their scorers. But now it was Sunderland who went into the semi-finals by the same score; both goals coming from defenders – Watson and Guthrie.

Arsenal, winners in 1971 and beaten finalists in 1972, were the semi-final opponents at Hillsborough. But the Londoners were destroyed in an arena too far north to be totally impartial. They gambled on the return of Blockley after injury, but the move failed when the expensive centre-half delivered a poor back-pass and Halom intercepted to score. Blockley was soon substituted but his height was missed when Hughes headed a second shortly after half-time. Though George pulled one back, Sunderland, by now 13th in Division Two, were at Wembley.

Leeds United's path to their ninth final in as many seasons had not been all serenity. Resolute Norwich City forced them to a second replay before an Allan Clarke hat-trick inside 15 minutes destroyed them, while Plymouth Argyle were only losers at Elland Road by the odd goal in three. But Plymouth's goal was the last to be scored against Leeds as they strode again into the final; West Bromwich Albion went down to two more Clarke goals, Derby lost to a typical Peter Lorimer drive, Wolves to an equally characteristic piece of poaching by Billy Bremner.

But only those in the immediate environs of the Yorkshire city wished for what seemed to be the inevitable act of Leeds retaining the Cup. Certainly the romance of the Sunderland story had captured the hearts of the neutrals. But it was not just a case of the predictable support for a David in the struggle against a Goliath; for many it was also a battle of good against

138

bad, with Leeds cast in the role of the villains.

For if Leeds United had established a reputation as the most consistent British club, they were certainly the most criticised, both from within and without the game. The main charge was of cynical play, such as feigning injuries to disrupt the pattern of play of opposing sides, or continually pressurising referees, or, in the dressing-room vernacular, of having a large number of players, defenders and attackers alike, who could 'look after themselves'. Indeed, Bob Stokoe went into print during the very week of the final claiming that Leeds had been up to tricks in ensuring that they had been allocated the dressing-room that they wanted and a more favoured end for their supporters to stand – charges which in fact could not be substantiated.

Nevertheless, the final represented a strange dichotomy for many an onlooker; whereas the heart almost bled for a Sunderland win, the head insisted that Leeds would inevitably perform their execution. A feeling accentuated when Leeds announced 12 players, of whom only Trevor Cherry had not played international football – a squad which also included Eddie Gray, restricted by injury to only five League games since November, but who had found Wembley's wide open spaces very much to his liking on his previous visits to the ground with Leeds and with Scotland. Sunderland could boast no more than that they were to be at full strength.

Saturday May 5 1973 began in disappointing fashion. Heavy morning downpours made the pitch glisten, but beneath the grass it was soft and yielding. The ball would skid through, making the weighting of passes and the retaining of balance feats of skill. The weather belonged to the past month, and the showers would continue throughout the afternoon.

As the teams came out Stokoe won yet another small victory with the crowd, not that he needed to do so, so popular had Sunderland become. Whilst Don Revie predictably sported his lucky grey suit, Stokoe wore the same red tracksuit as his players, emphasising the close relationship between the leader and the led.

Those who feared that Sunderland would be completely over-run must have been impressed with what they witnessed in the early moments of the match. The underdogs settled quickly, keeping what nerves they must have been feeling very much under the surface. More important in those formative minutes, it was evident that they had been well prepared to cope with the threat of Gray, whose skills in theory would be even more deadly on the wet turf which so suits the gifted dribbler.

As Giles, Bremner, and others, sensing their strength, fed a succession of passes to their left-winger, Sunderland revealed their organisation. Malone was never left unattended in face-to-face confrontation with Gray; Kerr, at 5ft 4½in arguably one of the smallest men to captain a team in a final, became his defensive henchman, always there to provide the first challenge or to cover. In those vital opening gambits Gray managed to slip one or the other but never both, and his threat to Sunderland never materialised.

While Malone and Kerr were coping admirably on the right, Watson and Pitt were doing the same in the centre of the defence. Almost from the whistle they established a supremacy in the air over Clarke and Jones that was almost startling. And when Clarke's fluency on the ground created some danger, Watson showed that his size in no way made him statuesque by contriving two nimble rescuing tackles. While in front of the defence the wasp-like Horswill stung away at Bremner and Giles with no trace of the inferiority complex that he might have understandably revealed.

Indeed, the preliminary jousts provided such absorbing viewing that no-one noticed the fact that 20 minutes elapsed before the first real shot at goal. Then it was Sunderland and the abrasive Horswill who pulled the trigger; the midfield man's controlled right-footer from 20 yards skidded low past Harvey's goal with the goalkeeper beaten. And if Leeds' method ensured them of more possession it was again Harvey who had the next awkward moment just on the half hour. Kerr, always willing to forsake his patrolling of Gray when Sunderland had the ball, aimed a deep cross from the right towards Halom but overhit drastically. On a dry day the ball, arriving just below crossbar height, would have provided Harvey with a comfortable catch. But aware of its slipperiness he opted for safety, turning it behind for a corner on Sunderland's left.

It was the signal for Watson to stride forward to add his dangerous forehead to Sunderland's artillery, and predictably he was the target as Hughes took the corner. The Leeds defenders were all too well aware of Watson's potential in the air, and as the ball arched towards the far post where the big centre-half was moving to meet it, their prior concern was to quash that threat. The net result was that Watson and two white-shirted opponents all missed the cross, and the ball continued its arc beyond the far post where it struck a somewhat surprised Halom. Off balance, the muscular striker could do no more than divert it back across goal, past where Watson and his markers were struggling to regain their equilibrium. It reached Ian Porterfield, who brought order to the bouncing ball by killing it with his left thigh. No Leeds defender moved as the Sunderland number 10 snaked out his right foot and volleyed cleanly over Harvey and just under the crossbar. Thirty-one minutes had passed and David had struck the first blow against all the odds.

If Sunderland's lead was remarkable, nothing was more incredible than the method by which Porterfield finished the job. His was perhaps the most famed left foot on the field, so sharp and sure that he could open a can of beans with it. But he was the first to admit that he takes his right foot on the field to stand on while he is wielding the left like a rapier. So sweetly did he strike the volley that his left foot would have been proud of the effort.

It took Leeds through the half-time interval and the wise counsel of Don Revie to recoil from that blow, and they began the second half in their most impressive vein. Reaney and Cherry stormed up and down the flanks to add their support to the assault, but the end product was usually a cross, and the heads of Watson and Pitt or the hands of Montgomery were equal to the aerial bombardment. Once Bremner wriggled into a shooting position, but when Montgomery could not hold the ball Malone reacted smartly and heaved it to safety.

It was Bremner, too, who had cause to complain when Mr

Burns, the referee, turned down animated appeals for a penalty when it looked as though one of Watson's telescopic legs had tripped the Leeds captain. In the referee's defence, he was beautifully positioned but a few yards from the incident, and certainly Bremner's topple in flamboyant style might have disguised some of the legality of the claim.

But such breaches in Sunderland's composure were rare, and Malone and Kerr so dispirited Gray with their vigilance that the Scottish International gave way to a Welsh International, Yorath. As the minutes ticked away Leeds struggled to retain their method and composure as the sense of desperation and frustration increased. Then, midway through the second half, came the moment when they must have realised that it was not to be their day.

As yet another cross was slung into the Sunderland goalmouth, the willing Cherry, sprinting in towards the far post, flung himself forward to fashion a magnificent diving header. Montgomery, across his goal to cover that post, reacted swiftly to parry the effort but he could not hold it. The millions of hearts that had fallen in love with Sunderland stood still as the ball rolled invitingly across the empty goal into the path of Lorimer, a reliable finisher at short as well as long range.

There was no panic from Lorimer, no careless reaction at being presented with a gilt-edged chance of saving Leeds. He met the ball solidly with his powerful right-foot and drove it at goal, turning away as he hit it, certain in his own mind that he had equalised. Just how Montgomery reached the shot only he will ever know, but reach it he did in a blur of green, and making a strong enough contact with his left wrist to turn the ball up on to the crossbar. Only the Sunderland player who cleared it knows what happened as it dropped; the Leeds players and the crowd were stunned in disbelief at Montgomery's breathtaking agility.

Though Leeds maintained pressure to the end, it never matched that ferocious fervour again, and Halom, in a breakaway might have scored a second for Sunderland. When the final whistle went it was to Montgomery that Stokoe ran in uninhibited rapture, while Don Revie was left to contemplate yet again the desolation of coming second, this time to the first Second Division side to win the FA Cup for 42 years. Sunderland, the winners in '37 had become winners in '73, and for all the romance of such a fairy-tale occasion, Revie would almost certainly be amongst those who believed that fate had intended it all the way along.